Praise for *Designing with Sound*

"Designing with Sound *is a broad and accessible introduction
to the design process for making interfaces that are calmer, less
intrusive, and more human friendly. This book helped me think
differently about sound in day-to-day life. It broadened my
vocabulary, and made me a better listener."*

TOBY NELSON, PROGRAMMER/MUSICIAN

*"I'm a voice, interaction and product designer, designing experiences
on physical devices from wearables to autonomous vehicles; sound
plays a crucial role in the design of a holistic experience. This book
gives designers a foundation to understand sound, and then the
process for design. A must read."*

**KAREN KAUSHANSKY, PRODUCT DESIGNER
SPECIALIZING IN VOICE/AUDIO, CONSULTANT**

*"I believe this to be a pioneering effort. It connects sound with
products and experiences in a way that makes it hard for future
books to stand shoulder to shoulder with this one. It takes a career of
decades to be able to write this."*

PETER SIKKING, INTERACTION DESIGNER

Designing with Sound

Fundamentals for Products and Services

Amber Case and Aaron Day

Beijing · Boston · Farnham · Sebastopol · Tokyo

Designing with Sound
by Amber Case and Aaron Day

Published by O'Reilly Media, Inc., 1005 Gravenstein Highway North, Sebastopol, CA 95472.

O'Reilly books may be purchased for educational, business, or sales promotional use. Online editions are also available for most titles (*http://oreilly.com/safari*). For more information, contact our corporate/institutional sales department: (800) 998-9938 or *corporate@oreilly.com*.

Acquisitions Editor: Jessica Haberman
Development Editor: Angela Rufino
Production Editor: Melanie Yarbrough
Copyeditor: Rachel Monaghan
Proofreader: Rachel Head
Indexer: Lucie Haskins

Cover Designer: Karen Montgomery
Interior Designers: Ron Bilodeau and Monica Kamsvaag
Illustrators: Rebecca Panzer
Compositor: Melanie Yarbrough

November 2018: First Edition.

Revision History for the First Edition:

2018-11-13   First release

See *http://oreilly.com/catalog/errata.csp?isbn=0636920051923* for release details.

978-1-491-96110-0

[LSI]

Designing with Sound

Fundamentals for Products and Services

Amber Case and Aaron Day

Beijing · Boston · Farnham · Sebastopol · Tokyo

Designing with Sound
by Amber Case and Aaron Day

Copyright © 2019, Amber Case and Aaron Day. All rights reserved.

Published by O'Reilly Media, Inc., 1005 Gravenstein Highway North, Sebastopol, CA 95472.

O'Reilly books may be purchased for educational, business, or sales promotional use. Online editions are also available for most titles (*http://oreilly.com/safari*). For more information, contact our corporate/institutional sales department: (800) 998-9938 or *corporate@oreilly.com*.

Acquisitions Editor: Jessica Haberman
Development Editor: Angela Rufino
Production Editor: Melanie Yarbrough
Copyeditor: Rachel Monaghan
Proofreader: Rachel Head
Indexer: Lucie Haskins

Cover Designer: Karen Montgomery
Interior Designers: Ron Bilodeau and Monica Kamsvaag
Illustrators: Rebecca Panzer
Compositor: Melanie Yarbrough

November 2018: First Edition.

Revision History for the First Edition:

> 2018-11-13   First release

See *http://oreilly.com/catalog/errata.csp?isbn=0636920051923* for release details.

978-1-491-96110-0

[LSI]

[*contents*]

[*contents*]

PART I   **PRINCIPLES AND PATTERNS OF SOUND DESIGN**

Preface

Why Sound Design Is Critical to Successful Products

For something so key to the human experience, we have few words to describe the types of sound available to us. This is why we often see user-centered sound design fall by the wayside, leaving customers with detractive results. This book is designed to bridge gaps in terminology and illuminate aspects of sound and sound design. A well-designed interface using sound can be profoundly effective, conveying nuance as well as emotion and urgency, without adding to the visual clutter that characterizes modern technology. We have many benchmarks and concepts for visual design. It is important for us to have frameworks and terminology for sound design as well. With better guidelines, technology can be more calming and human-centered.

WHY DOES SOUND MATTER?

Sound is emotional

> Because hearing is passive and immediate, it is capable of producing an emotional response irrespective of the intention of the human experiencing it. Music and voice can affect our emotions directly and without interpretation. The sound of light rain falling on a summer day can elicit a sense of calm and ease. Listen to Amália Rodrigues singing "Estranha Forma de Vida" and see if you can resist slipping into melancholy, even if you do not understand the words.

Sound is informative

> Many of our responses to sound are hardwired by our physiology. These innate responses range from momentary distraction to delight to a fight-or-flight response.

Sound is a powerful brand differentiator

Well implemented, sound allows a product to stand out; poorly implemented, it detracts. Just as with a visual user interface, sound should cultivate a consistent impression across products and platforms. Auditory cues can be subtle, leaving us without a distinct impression of any one sound, but when they complement the other aspects of design, they can leave us with a deep sense of satisfaction and cohesion. This can produce a successful brand identity.

Sound can ease cognitive burdens

We build more and more products every year, and our environments are more the result of human than natural processes. Our attention is already overloaded, and rather than taking some of the cognitive load off our beleaguered brains, undesigned sounds often add to the burden. Digital recording and playback marks an advancement over analog instruments in that it lets us produce and share music even more easily. But this ease of access comes with drawbacks, such as the loss of communal listening and the loss of sound quality due to compression. Today it is rare to hear full, natural music as we might in a chamber music hall. Instead, we most often hear music that is processed so it can be listenable at low bit rates, making it relatively easy to stream, but diminished in terms of quality. This places a hidden cognitive burden on our brains, which must work to fill minuscule gaps in the music left by the compression process. This is the pragmatic argument for improving our sound design capabilities. With better sound and less compressed audio, we can create more productivity with less effort.

Sound impacts productivity

We have evolved to expect a certain level of background noise, and a certain level of variability: nature is rarely silent, but it is also rarely loud, and loud noises in nature often indicate danger. Because of this, sound can impact our behavior and productivity in a dramatic way. It is difficult to focus on a task when part of your brain is sensing danger, but it is also easy to dismiss these effects when no actual danger is present. For these reasons, sound has an extraordinary ability to influence our experience of tasks, promoting or sapping concentration, creativity, and resolve.

This book is written to be useful to anyone who wants to design or improve on the auditory experience of a new or existing product. It is for anyone who needs to determine when, where, or how sounds are used. From executives to product managers, designers, and developers, and from entrepreneurs to integrated device manufacturers, this book is intended to be the introduction to sound design that non–sound engineers can put to use. We hope it will lead to a better sonic experience for all of us.

The Subjective Nature of Sound

The first step to designing sound is to have a solid understanding of how sound works. We can draw on this knowledge to use sound in products, experiences, and environments (adding, changing, or removing it) in a way that is better for everyone.

Many references speak mainly about the physical phenomena of sound, while we are almost certainly thinking of sound in subjective terms— how we perceive it. When a reference switches back and forth between objective, physical concepts (like sound pressure level, wavelengths, and frequency) and subjective, perceptual ideas (like loudness and pitch) without indicating that it is doing so, the entire subject becomes muddled. In this book, we try to explicitly call out the objective and the subjective aspects of sound.

Audio engineering is complex and challenging because it must work with the distortions introduced by our unique auditory faculties. Some of the frustration between sound engineers and their clients may stem from the fact that these complexities are not commonly understood outside of the field. References often discuss sound as if it were as simple as compressions of air with different strengths and different frequencies, but when it comes to how we hear sound, this is simply not the case.

Our hearing treats the physical phenomena of sound as though interpreted through a funhouse mirror. Sounds of the same physical energy (sound pressure waves, measured in decibels) are heard as differing in loudness depending on their frequency. The same frequency is perceived as a different pitch depending on how loud it is. Sounds that are short enough don't sound like tones at all, but instead sound like a "click." All of this becomes confusing when we are trying to talk about sound.

Learning How to Listen

Anyone who makes decisions about how something sounds should be equipped with good listening skills. How else will they be able to put themselves in the shoes of their customers? Listening is a skill that needs to be learned. It takes time and conscious effort. Practice listening to your environment. Understanding music can certainly help you design better, but it is important to pay attention to sounds in your environment.

Recording sound will allow you to gather a more sophisticated palette to work with. Record the little things in life: the sound of footsteps in a hallway with carpet and without, what voices sound like in a restaurant with a lot of reverb, or the sounds that children make versus adults. Record lawn mowers, engines, and dogs; boats and cars and weather. See what it sounds like when you record a car from behind a concrete wall versus right next to it. See how machines sound different from different angles, and whether you are closer to the source or farther away from it.

You can use a digital recorder (Figure P-1) or record on a phone with an app, using *.wav* or *.aiff* format. This is important because, unlike *.mp3* files, which compress the audio, *.wav* and *.aiff* files are larger, are higher resolution, and can give you a much better understanding of sound during recording and a visual display of the sound waves. Some mobile apps, like Twisted Wave Recorder, allow for recording and playback. Record at a high resolution of 44.1 KHz. Download free software like Audacity or WavePad. Then play with recording!

Remember that, while hearing is passive, *listening* is an active experience. Being able to listen and not just hear is one of the skills that distinguish a truly effective designer.

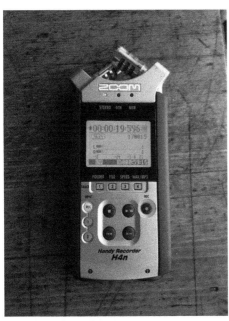

FIGURE P-1

A Zoom brand digital recorder (image courtesy Aaron Day)

Sound should work with us, not against us. The best technologies get out of our way and let us live our lives. As the world gets noisier, a greater understanding of how sound affects us is more and more important. When we *design* sound instead of just *including* it in our projects, we're improving the auditory experience for all who come into contact with our work. Hopefully this book will teach you how to understand, work with, and improve the auditory experience and how crucial it can be for products in everyday life. If you'd like to learn more, visit *designingwithsound.com*, Amber Case's site at *caseorganic.com* and *calmtech.com*, and Aaron Day's site at *aaron-day.com*. Be curious. Be patient. Be brave. Listen.

Let's begin!

How This Book Is Organized

PART 1: PRINCIPLES AND PATTERNS OF SOUND DESIGN

Chapter 1, Opportunities in Sound Design

This chapter covers past, present, and upcoming advances in sound design—including leveraging sound's effect on our sense of taste and using sound to provide wireless power—and discusses other overlooked areas of how sound can enhance our relationship with the world.

Chapter 2, Subtractive Sound Design for Products

This chapter covers techniques and principles of designing quieter products, starting with innovations pioneered by the automotive industry. Topics span from creating a good fit between components, minimizing unoccupied space, and adding sound-absorbing materials to adding containers and Helmholtz cavities to dampen sounds. The chapter finishes with a discussion of how vibration and turbulence can add unwanted sound to products, and how to design products in a way that reduces these sources of noise.

Chapter 3, Adding Sound to Interactions

A good sound designer knows when to add and when to take away. This chapter covers a set of guidelines for adding sounds to interactions, which can be done with the aim of improving the user experience, augmenting displays, or enhancing environments.

Chapter 4, Removing Sound from Interactions

This chapter covers a set of guidelines for removing sounds from interactions. At times, reducing sound in the interaction is the best way to improve the user experience of a product. This approach can often save costs by reducing development time for new sounds. Knowing when to take away can be an extremely effective skill.

Chapter 5, Sound and Brand

This chapter provides some guidelines for creating and working with sound and brand for both physical and digital products. Anything that produces sound is an extension of a brand, including keystroke sounds, the acoustics of tapping on a device, and what it sounds like to drop, unwrap, or use a device.

Chapter 6, Designing Voice Interfaces

This chapter covers how to design a voice persona and other considerations for the voice in voice interfaces.

PART 2: THE SOUND DESIGN PROCESS

Chapter 7, Interviewing

This chapter covers how best to interview stakeholders, engineers, and anyone else involved in the development process.

Chapter 8, Design

This chapter provides an overview of how to create a deliverable table and design document. The audit process helps you discover limits, landscape, and opportunities for design. You'll learn how to specify your design, and get buy-in on deliverables.

Chapter 9, Prototyping

It is often faster and less expensive to test sounds before they are put into the final product. This chapter provides an overview of some helpful prototyping methods, such as interactive palettes, video with sound overlays, video with paper prototypes, animation, and real-world prototypes.

Chapter 10, Hardware Testing

Once a prototype is made, it should be tested. Testing helps evaluate not just the performance, but the character of the audio hardware as well. This chapter covers how to test target hardware, what issues you might encounter and how to solve them, as well as final tuning and synchronization.

Chapter 11, User Testing

This chapter covers methods that can help inform, change, and validate design ideas, as well as research, preproduct testing, prototype testing, in-person and contextual. User testing in context is crucial for the success of sound design projects.

Vocabulary

We have found that a basic overview of the definitions of terms is one of the fastest ways to make people new to sound more comfortable discussing the topic. Consider this a brief sampling of different topics in sound. We have intentionally de-alphabetized the glossary terms in order to make them more accessible and enjoyable to read. We hope the reader will get far more use out of the book because they have these definitions in mind and can refer back to them if needed. The definitions are excerpted from J. Gordon Holt's *Audio Glossary* (Audio Amateur Press), with permission.

QUALITIES OF SOUND

qualifier

An adjective which the listener attaches to an observed sonic imperfection (such as "peaky" or "muddy") in order to convey a sense of its magnitude. "Subtle" and "conspicuous" are qualifying adjectives. See "audibility."

sheen

A rich-sounding overlay of velvety-smooth airiness or guttiness. A quality of outstanding high-frequency smoothness and ease.

rosinous (or resinous)

Describes the "zizzy" quality of bowed strings, particularly of cellos or violas.

gutty

Rosinous.

bloom

A quality of expansive richness and warmth, like the live body sound of a cello.

presence

A quality of realism and aliveness.

body

A quality of roundness and robustness in reproduced sound. "Gutsiness."

gutsy

Ballsy.

cool

Moderately deficient in body and warmth, due to progressive attenuation of frequencies below about 150Hz.

cold

The same as "cool," only more so. Having somewhat excessive upper-range output and weak lower-range output.

thin

Very deficient in bass. The result of severe attenuation of the range below 500 Hz.

sparse

Less cold than "pinched" but more than "thin."

thick

Describes sodden or heavy bass.

turgid

Thick.

clean

Free from audible distortion.

body sound

Of a musical instrument: the characteristic sound of the material of which the instrument is made, due to resonances of that material. The wooden quality of a viola, the "signature" by which a brass flute is distinguishable from a wooden or platinum one.

euphonic

Pleasing to the ear. In audio, "euphonic" has a connotation of exaggerated richness rather than literal accuracy.

dissonant

Unpleasant to the ear; ugly-sounding. Dissonance is an imperfection only when the music is not supposed to sound dissonant. Compare "consonant."

consonant

Agreeable to the ear; pleasant-sounding. Compare "dissonant."

smooth

Sound reproduction having no irritating qualities; free from high-frequency peaks, easy and relaxing to listen to. Effortless. Not necessarily a positive system attribute if accompanied by a slow, uninvolving character.

tipped-up

Having a rising high-frequency response.

toppy, toppish

Tipped-up. Slightly "tizzy" or "zippy."

zippy

A slight top-octave emphasis. See "toppy, toppish."

hot

Very tipped-up high frequencies.

golden

A euphonic coloration characterized by roundness, richness, sweetness, and liquidity.

haze, haziness

A moderate smearing of detail and focus. The audible equivalent of viewing something through a gauzy veil or a dirty window.

sweet

Having a smooth, softly delicate high end.

treacly

British for syrupy.

chocolatey

Like "syrupy," but darker and more full-bodied.

syrupy

Excessively sweet and rich, like maple syrup.

aggressive

Reproduced sound that is excessively forward and bright.

muffled

Very dull-sounding; having no apparent high frequencies at all. The result of high-frequency roll-off above about 2 kHz.

coarse

A large-grained texturing of reproduced sound; very gritty. The continuum of reproduced sound seems to be comprised of large particles. See "texture."

grunge

Sonic dirt, crud, roughness. Muffled grittiness.

liquid

Textureless sound.

glassy

Very bright.

harsh

Gratingly unpleasant to the ear.

texture, texturing

A perceptible pattern or structure in reproduced sound, even if random in nature. Texturing gives the impression that the energy continuum of the sound is composed of discrete particles, like the grain of a photograph.

rough

A quality of moderate grittiness, often caused by LP mistracking.

gritty

A harsh, coarse-grained texturing of reproduced sound. The continuum of energy seems to be composed of discrete, sharp-edged particles.

grainy

A moderate texturing of reproduced sound. The sonic equivalent of grain in a photograph. Coarser than dry but finer than gritty.

dry

1) Describing the texture of reproduced sound: very fine-grained, chalky. 2) Describing an acoustical space: deficient in reverberation or having a very short reverberation time. 3) Describing bass quality: lean, overdamped.

spiky

Pertains to a coarse texturing of sound characterized by the presence of many rapidly recurring sharp clicks. Like the sound of tearing cloth, only crisper.

chalky

Describes a texturing of sound that is finer than grainy but coarser than dry. See "texture."

snap

A quality of sound reproduction giving an impression of great speed and detail.

slam

(British) Impact.

boomy

Characterized by pronounced exaggeration of the midbass and, often, dominance of a narrow range of bass frequencies. See "one-note bass."

naturalness

Realism.

sodden, soggy

Describes bass that is loose and ill-defined. Woolly.

woolly

Pertains to loose, ill-defined bass.

loose

Pertains to bass which is ill-defined and poorly controlled. Woolly.

lush

Rich-sounding and sumptuous to the point of excess.

open

Exhibiting qualities of delicacy, air, and fine detail. Giving an impression of having no upper-frequency limit.

billowy (also "billowing")

Excessively reverberant.

plummy

(British) Fat, rich, lush-sounding.

airy

Pertaining to treble which sounds light, delicate, open, and seemingly unrestricted in upper extension. A quality of reproducing systems having very smooth and very extended high-frequency response.

dynamic

Giving an impression of wide dynamic range; punchy. This is related to system speed as well as to volume contrast.

congested

Smeared, confused, muddy, and flat. Totally devoid of transparency.

sock

A quality of sound reproduction giving a sensation of concussive impact.

visceral

Producing a bodily sensation of pressure or concussion.

sizzly

Emphasis of the frequency range above about 8kHz, which adds sibilance to all sounds, particularly those of cymbals and vocal esses (sibilants).

clinical

Sound that is pristinely clean but wholly uninvolving.

silvery

Sound that is slightly hard or steely, but clean.

steely

Shrill. Like "hard," but more so.

hard

Tending toward steeliness, but not quite shrill. Often the result of a moderate frequency-response hump centered around 6kHz, sometimes also caused by small amounts of distortion.

closed-in

Lacking in openness, delicacy, air, and fine detail. A closed-in sound is usually caused by high-frequency roll-off above 10kHz. Compare with "open," "airy."

lean

Very slightly bass-shy. The effect of a very slight bass roll-off below around 500Hz. Not quite "cool."

soft

Very closed-in, markedly deficient at the extreme high end.

opaque

Lacking detail and transparency.

pristine

Very clean-sounding, very transparent.

strident

Unpleasantly shrill, piercing.

shrill

Strident, steely.

silky

Pertains to treble performance that is velvety-smooth, delicate, and open.

screechy

The ultimate stridency, akin to chalk on a blackboard or a razor blade being scraped across a windowpane.

muddy

Ill-defined, congested.

tubby

Having an exaggerated deep-bass range.

vague, vagueness

Having poor specificity, confused.

velvet fog (as in "listening through a...")

Describes a galloping case of haze, wherein virtually all detail and focus are absent.

LISTENING TO SOUND

acuity

1) The sensitivity of the ears to very soft sounds. 2) The acquired ability of an audiophile to hear and to assess the subtle qualitative attributes of reproduced sound.

audibility

The measure of the severity of a sonic imperfection. The scale of audibility, from least audible to most audible, is: inaudible, subtle, slight, moderate, obvious, conspicuous, and Arrggh!!

noticeable

In aural perception, any sonic quality which is clearly audible to most people.

perceptible

At or above the threshold of audibility of a trained listener.

subtle

Barely perceptible on a very good system. See "audibility."

inaudible

A sonic imperfection which is either too subtle to be consciously perceived or is actually nonexistent. Compare "subliminal."

subliminal

Too faint or too subtle to be consciously perceived. Compare "inaudible." See "listening fatigue."

slight

Easily audible on a good system but not necessarily on a lesser one. See "audibility."

moderate

A qualifier which describes a sonic imperfection which is clearly audible through any decent system, but not annoyingly so. See "audibility."

dramatic

Describing a perceived difference between components: very noticeable, unmistakable. A term misused by audio reviewers to demonstrate how incredibly sensitive they are to barely audible differences. See "audibility."

observation

The perceived attribute of a sonic element, on which a personal judgment about its quality is based. Observations are described by subjective terms such as "smooth," "woolly," or "spacious."

quality

The degree to which the reproduction of sound is judged to approach the goal of perfection.

involvement

The degree to which a reproduction draws the listener in to the musical performance and evokes an emotional response to it.

musical, musicality

A personal judgment as to the degree to which reproduced sound resembles live music. Real musical sound is both accurate and euphonic, consonant and dissonant.

phasey

A quality of reproduced sound which creates a sensation of pressure in the ears, unrelated to the intensity of the sound. Phasiness is experienced by many people when listening to two loudspeakers which are connected out of phase with each other.

cocktail party effect

The auditory system's controllable ability to separate out, on the basis of direction alone, one sound source from many coming from different directions. This allows you to follow one voice among the others at a noisy cocktail party.

precedence effect

The tendency for the ears to identify the source of a sound as being in the direction from which it is first heard.

imagery

Descriptive terminology intended to convey an impression or mental image of a subjective observation. Imagery is usually employed to describe qualities in reproduced sound in terms of more familiar sensory responses like vision, taste, and touch.

articulation

1) Clarity and intelligibility, usually of voice reproduction. 2) The reproduction of inner detail in complex sounds, which makes it easy to follow an individual musical voice among many.

palpable

Describes reproduction that is so realistic you feel you could reach out and touch the instruments or performers.

aliveness

A quality of sound reproduction which gives an impression that the performers are present, in person, in the listening room.

COMPONENTS OF SOUND

characteristic

One of the basic properties of reproduced sound, which contributes to its perceived quality. Frequency response, loudness, extension, soundstaging, and resolution are sonic characteristics.

element

One of the constituent parts of a sonic characteristic. Bass, mid-range, and treble are elements of frequency response. Depth and breadth are elements of soundstaging.

click

A small, sharp impulse that sounds like the word "click."

impulse

An abrupt, extremely brief burst of signal energy; a transient.

crackle

Intermittent medium-sized clicks. The usual background noise from much-played vinyl discs.

buzz

A low-frequency sound having a spiky or fuzzy character.

attack

1) The buildup of sound when an instrument is bowed, blown, struck, or plucked. 2) The ability of a system to reproduce the attack transients in musical sound. Poor attack makes a system sound slow.

attack transient

The initial energy pulse of a percussive sound, such as from a piano string, triangle, or drum head.

transient

See "attack transient."

detail

The most subtle, delicate parts of the original sound, which are usually the first things lost by imperfect components. See "low-level detail." Compare "haze," "smearing," "veiling."

low-level detail

The subtlest elements of musical sound, which include the delicate details of instrumental sounds and the final tail of reverberation decay. See "delicacy."

delicacy

The reproduction of very subtle, very faint details of musical sound, such as the fingertip-friction sounds produced when a guitar or a harp is played. See "low-level detail."

sonic detail

See "detail."

impulse noise

Transient noise, such as surface-noise ticks and pops.

noise

Any spurious background sounds, usually of a random or indeterminate pitch: hiss, crackles, ticks, pops, whooshes.

decay

The reverberant fadeout of a musical sound after it has ceased. Compare "attack."

FREQUENCY RANGE

Organized by ascending frequency.

frequency range

A range of frequencies stated without level limits: i.e., "The upper bass covers the frequency range 80–160Hz."

frequency (or amplitude) response

1) A range of frequencies stated with level limits: i.e., "The woofer's response was 20–160Hz ±3dB." 2) The uniformity with which a system or individual component sounds as if it reproduces the range of audible frequencies. Equal input levels at all frequencies should be reproduced by a system with subjectively equal output.

infrasonic

Below the range of audible frequencies. Although inaudible, the infrasonic range from 15–20Hz can be felt if strongly reproduced. Compare "subsonic."

subsonic

Slower than the speed of sound through air. Often used incorrectly to mean "infrasonic."

low frequency

Any frequency lower than 160Hz.

bass

The range of frequencies below 160Hz, characterized by low pitch.

sub-bass

Infrasonic bass.

deep bass

Frequencies below 40Hz.

low bass

The range from 20–40Hz.

midbass

The range of frequencies from 40–80Hz.

upper bass

The range of frequencies from 80–160Hz.

midrange (also "middles")

The range of frequencies from 160–1300Hz.

lower middles

The range of frequencies from 160–320Hz.

upper middles

The range of frequencies from 650–1300Hz.

high-frequency range

1) The audio range above 1300Hz. 2) The usable upper limit of that range. See "extension."

treble

The frequency range above 1.3kHz.

presence range

The lower-treble part of the audio spectrum, approximately 1–3kHz, which contributes to presence in reproduced sound.

lower highs

The range of frequencies from 1.3–2.6kHz.

middle highs

> The range of frequencies from 2.6–5kHz.

upper highs

> The range of frequencies from 10–20kHz.

top

> The high treble, the range of audio frequencies above about 8kHz.

extreme highs

> The range of audible frequencies above 10kHz.

ultrasonic

> Beyond the upper-frequency limit of human hearing. Compare "supersonic."

supersonic

> Faster than the speed of sound through air. Sometimes used incorrectly to mean ultrasonic.

roll-off (also "rollout")

> A frequency response which falls gradually above or below a certain frequency limit. By comparison, the term "cutoff" (often abbreviated to "cut," as in "bass cut") implies an abrupt loss of level above or below the frequency limit.

COLORATION OF SOUND

vowel coloration

> A form of midrange or low-treble coloration which impresses upon all program material a tonal "flavor" resembling a vowel in speech.

coloration

> An audible "signature" with which a reproducing system imbues all signals passing through it.

neutral

> Free from coloration.

"ah" (rhymes with "rah")

> A vowel coloration caused by a frequency-response peak centered around 1000Hz.

honky

> Pertaining to a severe "aw" coloration.

"aw" (rhymes with "paw")

A vowel coloration caused by a frequency-response peak centered around 450Hz. An "aw" coloration tends to emphasize and glamorize the sound of large brass instruments (trombone, tuba).

horn sound

An "aw" coloration characteristic of many loudspeakers that have a horn-loaded midrange.

comb filtering (also "flanging," "phasing")

A hollow coloration that, once recognized, is unmistakable. Caused by a regularly spaced series of frequency-response peaks and dips, most often due to interference between two identical signals spaced in time. If that time difference is continually changed, the comb-filter peaks and dips move accordingly, giving rise to the familiar "phasing," "flanging," or "jet plane" effect used in modern rock music.

"ee" (rhymes with "we")

A vowel coloration caused by a frequency-response peak centered around 3.5kHz.

"eh" (as in "bed")

A vowel coloration caused by a frequency-response peak centered around 2kHz.

nasal

Reproduced sound having the quality of a person speaking with his/her nose blocked. Like the vowel "eh" coloration. In a loudspeaker, often due to a measured peak in the upper midrange followed by a complementary dip.

"ih" (as in "bit")

A vowel coloration caused by a frequency-response peak centered around 3.5kHz.

"oh" (as in "toe")

A vowel coloration caused by a broad frequency-response peak centered around 250Hz.

boxy

> 1) Characterized by an "oh" vowel coloration, as when speaking with one's head inside a box. 2) Used to describe the upper-bass/lower-midrange sound of a loudspeaker with excessive cabinet-wall resonances.

"oo" (as in "gloom")

> A vowel coloration caused by a broad frequency-response peak centered around 120Hz.

hooty

> 1) Pertaining to a severe "ooo" coloration. 2) Resonant colorations may cause some lower-midrange notes to jump forward or "hoot" at the listener.

pop

> A midrange pulse characterized by a very sharp attack followed by a short "o" or "aw" vowel sound. Usually the result of a severe LP blemish.

pinched

> 1) Very cold, with a "nyeah" coloration. 2) Pertaining to soundstaging: laterally compressed and lacking in spaciousness.

sibilance

> A coloration that resembles or exaggerates the vocal s-sound.

soundstaging, soundstage presentation

> The accuracy with which a reproducing system conveys audible information about the size, shape, and acoustical characteristics of the original recording space and the placement of the performers within it.

spitty

> An edgy "ts" coloration which exaggerates musical overtones and sibilants as well as LP surface noise. Usually the result of a sharp response peak in the upper treble range.

wiry

> Having an edgy or distorted high end, similar to the "tish" of brushed cymbals, but coloring all sounds reproduced by the system.

tizzy

A "zz" or "ff" coloration of the sound of cymbals and vocal sibilants, caused by a rising frequency response above 10kHz. Similar to "wiry," but at a higher frequency.

cupped-hands

A coloration reminiscent of someone speaking through cupped hands or, if extreme, a megaphone.

TECHNICAL ATTRIBUTES OF SOUND

definition

That quality of sound reproduction which enables the listener to distinguish between, and follow the melodic lines of, the individual voices or instruments comprising a large performing group.

resolution

See "definition."

extension

The usable limits of a component's frequency range.

reaction

A counterforce imparted to a speaker enclosure in response to the air resistance to the motion of a moving diaphragm or cone. On a thick carpet, a reacting enclosure will rock slightly back and forth, impairing low-frequency quality and overall detail.

dynamic range

1) Pertaining to a signal: the ratio between the loudest and the quietest passages. 2) Pertaining to a component: the ratio between its no-signal noise and the loudest peak it will pass without distortion.

damping

The amount of control an amplifier seems to impose on a woofer. Underdamping causes loose, heavy bass; overdamping yields very tight but lean bass.

strained

Showing signs of audible distress during loud passages, as though the system is verging on overload. Compare "ease," "effortless."

ease

Pertains to reproduction which sounds effortless, free from strain.

effortless

Unstrained; showing no signs of audible stress during loud passages. Compare "strained."

one-note bass

The exaggeration of a single bass note, due to a sharp low-frequency peak, normally due to an underdamped woofer but also caused by room resonances.

rotated

The sound of a frequency response that is linear but tilted.

monaural

Literally "hearing with one ear." Often used incorrectly in place of "monophonic" (as in Glenn D. White's otherwise excellent *Audio Dictionary*, 1991, second edition, University of Washington Press). Compare "binaural."

binaural

Literally hearing with "two ears," refers to a recording/playback system which presents the listener's ears with the acoustic waveforms they would have received at the original event. Only currently achievable with a "dummy-head" microphone and playback via headphones.

mono (also "monophonic")

A system or recording with one channel or speaker. See "monaural."

single-mono

Sound reproduction through a single loudspeaker system. Compare "dual mono."

double (or dual) mono

Reproduction of a monophonic signal through both channels/speakers of a stereo system, as when a preamplifier's mode switch is set to A+B (L+R). Compare "single mono."

stereo (also "stereophonic")

A two-channel recording or reproducing system. Compare "binaural," "monophonic." See "dual mono," "single mono."

distortion

1) Any unintentional or undesirable change in an audio signal.

2) An overlay of spurious roughness, fuzziness, harshness, or stridency in reproduced sound.

rounding (also "rounding-off")

The shearing-off of sharp attack transients, due to poor transient response or restricted high-frequency range. See "slow," "speed."

dip

A narrow area of depression within an otherwise flat frequency-response curve.

suckout

A deep, narrow frequency-response dip.

scrape flutter

Roughness and veiling of analog tape sound due to discontinuous movement of the tape across the head ("violining").

violining

See "scrape flutter."

veiled, veiling

Pertaining to a deficiency of detail and focus, due to moderate amounts of distortion, treble-range restriction, or attack rounding.

smearing

Severe lack of detail and focus.

discontinuity

A change of tone color (timbre) or coloration due to the signal's transition, in a multi-way speaker system, from one driver to another having dissimilar coloration.

slow

Sound reproduction which gives the impression that the system is lagging behind the electrical signals being fed to it. See "fast," "speed," "tracking."

speed

The apparent rapidity with which a reproducing system responds to steep wavefronts and overall musical pace. See "fast," "slow."

tracking

The degree to which a component responds to the dictates of the audio signal, without lag or overshoot.

bright, brilliant

The most often misused terms in audio, these describe the degree to which reproduced sound has a hard, crisp edge to it. Brightness relates to the energy content in the 4kHz–8kHz band. It is *not* related to output in the extreme-high-frequency range. All live sound has brightness; it is a problem only when it is excessive.

crisp

In reproduced sound: sharply focused and detailed, sometimes excessively so because of a peak in the mid-treble region.

dirty

Sound reproduction which is fuzzy, cruddy, or spiky.

fast

Giving an impression of extremely rapid reaction time, which allows a reproducing system to "keep up with" the signal fed to it. (A "fast woofer" would seem to be an oxymoron, but this usage refers to a woofer tuning that does not boom, make the music sound "slow," obscure musical phrasing, or lead to "one-note bass.") Similar to "taut," but referring to the entire audio-frequency range instead of just the bass.

quick

See "fast."

flat

1) Having a subjectively uniform frequency response, free from humps and dips. 2) Deficient in or lacking in soundstage depth, resulting in the impression that all reproduced sound sources are the same distance from the listener.

glare

An unpleasant quality of hardness or brightness, due to excessive low- or mid-treble energy.

O'Reilly Safari

Safari (formerly Safari Books Online) is a membership-based training and reference platform for enterprise, government, educators, and individuals.

Members have access to thousands of books, training videos, Learning Paths, interactive tutorials, and curated playlists from over 250 publishers, including O'Reilly Media, Harvard Business Review, Prentice Hall Professional, Addison-Wesley Professional, Microsoft Press, Sams, Que, Peachpit Press, Adobe, Focal Press, Cisco Press, John Wiley & Sons, Syngress, Morgan Kaufmann, IBM Redbooks, Packt, Adobe Press, FT Press, Apress, Manning, New Riders, McGraw-Hill, Jones &; Bartlett, and Course Technology, among others.

How to Contact Us

Please address comments and questions concerning this book to the publisher:

> O'Reilly Media, Inc.
> 1005 Gravenstein Highway North
> Sebastopol, CA 95472
> 800-998-9938 (in the United States or Canada)
> 707-829-0515 (international or local)
> 707-829-0104 (fax)

We have a web page for this book, where we list errata, examples, and any additional information. You can access this page at *http://bit.ly/designing-with-sound*.

To comment or ask technical questions about this book, send email to *bookquestions@oreilly.com*.

For more information about our books, courses, conferences, and news, see our website at *http://www.oreilly.com*.

Find us on Facebook: *http://facebook.com/oreilly*

Follow us on Twitter: *http://twitter.com/oreillymedia*

Watch us on YouTube: *http://www.youtube.com/oreillymedia*

Acknowledgments

To our primary content editors, Carl Alviani and Kellyn Yvonne Standley, for long days and nights of in-depth help, and to the fantastic and very patient Angela Rufino and Mary Treseler, our editors at O'Reilly: thank you. Thank you to Lynn Kimbrough for copy editing.

Thanks also to our patient and dedicated content reviewers: Toby Nelson, Jonathan H Brown, Nim Wunnan, James Nesfield, Joshua Marinacci, Xuehong Liu, Peter Sikking, Karen Kaushansky, Jess Mitchell, Alexander Baumgardt, Peter Bautista, Martyn Rowe, Dennis DeSantis, George Abraham, and Anselm Hook.

Amber Case would like to thank Toby Nelson for always believing in her, no matter the odds. She would like to thank her mom for giving her an early desire to learn; Sheldon Renan, for getting her to write books in the first place; Douglas Rushkoff, for his positive and constant encouragement; and Professor Deborah Heath, for getting her started in the field of studying humans and technology. Finally, she would like to thank her late father, Eliot Case, who passed away from cancer during the production of this book. He was a recording engineer, sound designer, and inventor. Her childhood memories of her father were filled with speakers, microphones, and synthesizers. She watched him constantly experiment with sounds and spaces. Although he did not live to see the final production of this book, it is her hope that it might make him proud.

Aaron Day would like to thank his wife, Cornelia, and son, Avo, for their encouragement and patience throughout this process. He would also like to thank Jim Flynn, Vance Galloway, and Bruce Christian Bennett for their wisdom, which started him on this path so long ago.

Part I

Principles and Patterns of Sound Design

Opportunities in Sound Design

THERE ARE MANY OPPORTUNITIES to improve the auditory experience in products. With additive sound, we can include sounds where there were none before, helping to change mood, increase energy, or instill a sense of calm. With subtractive sound, we can remove sound in whole or in part, making for quieter cafés, better-sounding conversations, and more pleasant products.

Sound plays an increasingly exciting role in product design, human–machine interaction, our buildings and spaces, and the quality of our notifications. We can use audio to deliver information in a way that visuals cannot, and there are many places to apply these skills. Expect to see innovations across different markets in the near future.

This chapter covers past, present, and upcoming advances in sound design and discusses often-overlooked areas where sound can enhance our relationship with the world. We begin by exploring how sound can affect our sense of taste.

Sound Design and Taste Modulation

It is a well-known fact that food tastes different in airplanes. Cabin noise actually alters your sense of taste. The low humming sounds reduce sweet and salty experiences, and amplify bitter and umami flavors (*umami* is a Japanese word that describes the fifth basic taste found in savory flavors, such as rich broths, meats, and shiitake mushrooms). These factors make food less tasty during air travel. This scientific theory, called taste modulation, reveals that high frequencies can heighten sweet flavors, while low frequencies can bring out bitter flavors.

To combat this, Finland's Ultra Nordic Agency worked with China's Master Chef Steven Liu and molecular gastronomy professor, Anu Hopia, to craft mealtime soundscapes for passengers on Finnair flights. The idea was to use elements of sound design, like the fact that high frequencies enhance our perception of sweetness, to restore some of food's tastiness in the air. The chef and gastronomist collaborated with sound designers to record Nordic landscapes and high-frequency ranges to match the food served on the flights. Passengers were given headphones and sounds to play during their meals.

After significant testing, researchers found that these passengers enjoyed a heightened dining experience, exhibiting a greater sense of taste with the soundtrack than without. The work was nominated for multiple awards at the 2018 International Sound Awards in Hamburg.

Restaurants and researchers are experimenting with the effects of sound on the palate, too. One London restaurant, House of Wolf (now closed), served a chocolate-covered bittersweet toffee with a phone number. Dialers were given an option of pressing 1 for sweet or 2 for bitter, and a soundtrack played that enhanced each taste accordingly. Other restaurants have considered how soundtracks might enhance the specific flavors of food. This principle could be applied to wine tastings, cafeteria food, and even health improvement efforts, such as using high frequencies as a substitute for high sugar content.[1]

Wireless Power Through Sound Waves

Using ultrasound, beamforming technology, optical lasers, and very specially designed transducers, Meredith Perry and her startup, uBeam, is innovating the remote transmission of energy through the air—using high-frequency sound outside of the range of human and animal hearing to beam power to wireless devices.[2] "Sound like sci-fi? uBeam is on the bleeding edge of technology, developing a system that wirelessly transports energy and data over distance through repetitive and precise vibration of the air—what we know as sound. Through our journey building this technology, I've fallen in love with the power of sound and its applicability across seemingly endless dimensions," says the founder.[3] The beam can work at up to 10 feet in line of the

---

1   Anne-Sylvie Crisinel and Charles Spence, "As Bitter as a Trombone: Synesthetic Correspondences in Nonsynesthetes Between Tastes/Flavors and Musical Notes," *Attention, Perception, & Psychophysics* 74, no. 7 (1994): 1994–2002, *https://www.ncbi.nlm.nih.gov/pubmed/20952795*.

2   Adam Grant, *In Originals*, page 122.

3   "The Power of Sound," *https://ubeam.com/Blog/the-power-of-sound/*

ultrasound beam, but they are working to expand the range further. Ultrasound has been used safely for nearly a century, and is extremely safe at very low power levels. There is no cumulative effect either, so it can work well for domestic applications. Accoding to Perry, "This is about a paradigm shift. If you're moving from your car to a coffee shop to work and your phone is charging while you're using it, it's no longer about what percentage you're at. You could stay at 1% all day."[4] The idea is that one day, hidden ultrasonic beaming stations could invisibly power any device in the IOT era (or "Internet of Things"), even electric vehicles. Running out of battery would be a thing of the past.

Additive Sound Design

Modern cars have engines that are so efficient, they no longer need to sound like they did in the '40s, '50s, and '60s. Most car sounds are designed in some way, from the *crumpf* of the door closing to the sound of acceleration. In fact, automobiles are one of the most carefully sound-designed products in the world, with many absorbing, diffracting, and vibration-isolating materials added to them to ensure a quiet ride at high speeds. After spending so many decades removing sounds and making cars quieter, however, vehicle manufacturers have had to design some sounds back in. Muscle cars and hot rods sound strange when they're quiet, so rich artificial engine sounds are designed, digitized, and piped in through vehicle speaker systems. Because engine noises are also an important safety mechanism for pedestrians, electric vehicles have artificially added engine noise and backing-up sounds to ensure that passersby hear them. Otherwise, the quietness of these efficient cars presents a potential safety hazard.

Subtractive Sound Design

The sounds from leaf blowers, large trucks, and microwaves interrupt human lives. Companies like Dyson and Blendtec invest millions in research for everyday products that produce less noise and reap the benefits in markets. Blendtec released a blender that was so quiet it could operate at volumes lower than a conversation, revolutionizing the sound of an everyday task. Dyson worked with materials scientists,

---

4 Marco della Cava, "uBeam's Meredith Perry shows her stealth wireless charging technology really works," USA Today, *http://bit.ly/2Jm3WY3.*

engineers, and sound designers to create a quieter, hair dryer, pushing the industry forward for the first time in decades. Sometimes the most important improvement that can be made on a product is to remove some of the beeps and tones it makes in order to create a more pleasant experience. Subtractive sound design can be applied to hundreds of everyday products and environments.

Sonification

In 1908, Hans Geiger and his grad student Walther Müller filled a tube with an inert gas low-pressure and applied high voltage. This device detects radiation by producing an auditory click when radioactive particles ionize the gas and make the tube momentarily conductive. This elegant solution allowed engineers to detect invisible radiation by making it audible, transforming an entire scientific practice by allowing scientists to measure alpha, beta and gamma radiation with a relatively cheap and robust device. The development of the Geiger counter remains one of the most successful and important steps in the history of *sonification*: the process of converting information into sound.

Sound is strong in ways that visuals are not. Sound is more quickly perceived than sight, touch, smell, or taste.[5] Results of many studies show that auditory reaction time is far faster than visual reaction time.[6] Your ears can unambiguously pick out differences that your visual sense might confuse. *New York Times* writer Amanda Cox used this idea to sonify the last few seconds of four different 2010 Olympic events.[7] Visually, it seemed unclear who crossed the finish line first, because the participants finished only a few milliseconds apart. By assigning a clear sound to the moment when each person crossed the finish line, however, Cox was able to create an audible story about who won.

Because sound is such an accurate way to discern differences, there are many opportunities to apply sonification to better understand our world. These kinds of systems can help turn dynamic datasets, such

---

5 "The Speed of Hearing," MED-EL, *https://blog.medel.com/the-speed-of-hearing/*.

6 See e.g. Jose Shelton and Gideon Praveen Kumar, "Comparison Between Auditory and Visual Simple Reaction Times," *Neuroscience and Medicine* 1, no. 1 (2010): 30–2, *https://www.scirp.org/journal/PaperInformation.aspx?PaperID=2689*.

7 Amanda Cox, "Fractions of a Second: An Olympic Musical," *The New York Times*, *https://nyti.ms/2yAwKY5*.

as stock market changes or news stories, into a less intrusive auditory sense. When done well, they can help inform professions that have an overwhelming amount of visual data to process, such as medical personnel or researchers. Sonification is beneficial for any application that overwhelms the visual sense, such as large datasets that exhibit patterns over periods of time longer than the average human attention span. Imagine being able to listen to an experiment to determine if it is going well instead of peering persistently through a microscope. Audio-based experiences could enable doctors and nurses, investors, and industrial workers to work without distraction. Sonification could also provide farmers, technicians, and factory workers with an intuitive feel or where things stand and where problems might be arising.

SONIFICATION AND INCOME DATA ON THE NEW YORK SUBWAY LINE

Brian Foo, a New York–based programmer and visual artist, used 2011 US Census data to sonify income differences along the route of the New York 2 train's 49 stations (see Figure 1-1). Foo used a total of 63 sounds for the composition, many of them from artists and musicians from areas along the subway line. He also included the NYC subway chime, a sound familiar to anyone riding the subway.

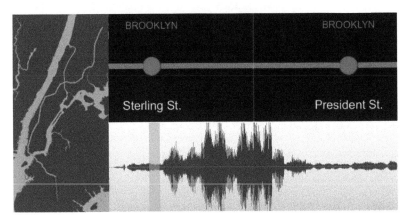

FIGURE 1-1
Sonification for the 2 train. The composition is minimal as the train starts toward downtown Manhattan. (Source: *https://vimeo.com/118358642*.)

The resulting composition matched the feeling of traveling along the subway, starting with a sensation of sleepiness as the train moves away from the city, followed by a feeling of excitement, and finally a sense of calming back down as the train leaves the city (see Figures 1-2 and 1-3).

FIGURE 1-2

The sound file for the 2 train reveals the overall compositional structure of the piece. (Source: *https://vimeo.com/118358642.*)

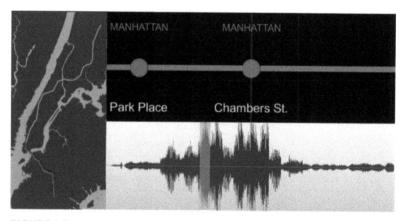

FIGURE 1-3

The soundscape of the 2 train entering Manhattan. The composition built up to more energy and complexity with the increase in income along the subway route. (Source: *https://vimeo.com/118358642.*)

Unlike many "fast" sonification methods, Foo used more instruments and a faster tempo for increases in income level, not pitch. He made sure to match the general composition to the data, with a flow that starts off relaxed and becomes more intense and "full" as the subway passes through the affluent financial district, and then thins out as it leaves Manhattan and enters the Bronx. It is possible to "feel" the income at each stop, and understand how it increases. The soundscape matches the visuals, the locations, and the dataset.

Foo strived to avoid assigning certain sounds to, or passing judgment on, income levels or neighborhoods. He wanted to keep the data presentation agnostic. Instead of positive or negative tones, he assigned more instruments and a faster tempo for higher income, and reduced the number of instruments and tempo with lower income.

Foo also used a method called *phase shifting*, a compositional approach pioneered in the 1960s by Terry Riley and Steve Reich in which two or more identical melodies are repeated with slightly variable tempos, so the melodies slowly shift in and out of sync with each other. Foo felt that this method provided the perfect metaphor for the NYC subway: "constantly looping but at different tempos, always running but never on time, phasing between order and chaos."[8] All 63 instruments and sounds used in the composition employ phase shifting.

SONIFICATION AND AGRICULTURE

We're able to glean a lot about our environment from simply listening to it, and we can learn from those soundscapes to design our own. Sonification could work alongside greenhouse sensors to indicate data necessary to ensure the health of plants. For example, the greenhouse could play a minimal soundscape to provide information on the overall balance of pH, nitrogen, or soil level. The data could then be converted into signal processing that would inform the caretakers so they can adjust the missing element rebalancing the system.

SONIFICATION AND STOCK TRADING

Sound is underutilized in the world of financial trading and there's an opportunity here for sound to inform and utilize peripheral attention. Day traders often work with multiple screens and a stressful visual channel. Even a pared-down, minimal display requires significant attention. Sonifying important information in the market can help reduce this visual burden.

---

8 Brian Foo, "Two Trains," Data-Driven DJ, *https://datadrivendj.com/tracks/subway/*.

Sound can help with emotional monitoring, too. Intense emotional swings can cause traders to panic and make poor decisions. Sound can notify traders when their heart and breathing rate, blood pressure, or galvanic skin response might signal an unreliable emotional state, potentially saving both money and emotional pain.

Sonification could also alert traders when patterns of price changes that occur in one group of correlated equities might affect the probability of high-volume trading in another. Because sound can be monitored passively, trading sonification could relieve investors from having to constantly check back and forth between monitors to review the trends, and mitigate the cognitive cost of reading visual displays.

Sound Design and Calm Technology

Calm Technology was a framework developed by Xerox PARC researchers Mark Weiser and John Seely Brown in the early 1990s as a way of reducing the cognitive impact of information on the human brain. Technology can provide information to help us make decisions, and the way in which it does so can be overwhelming or polite (i.e., calm). Weiser wrote that we need smarter humans, not smarter devices. He predicted that attention would be the scarcest resource in the future, and how technology draws on attention would make or break our interactions with it. The way to achieve a sense of calm is by informing without drawing attention away from the current task. Making technology calm is a matter of empowering the periphery.

If good design is about getting you to your goal with the fewest moves, calm technology is about getting you to your goal *with the least amount of attention* (see Figure 1-4).

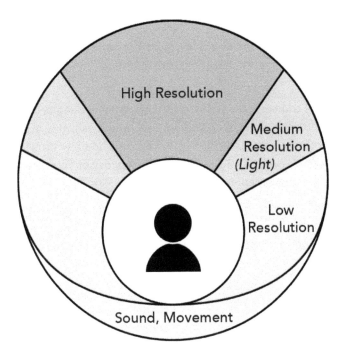

Areas of Attention

FIGURE 1-4

The areas of attention around a person. Primary denotes high-resolution attention—good for desktop computing, mobile technology, and other tasks that demand full attention. Secondary denotes medium resolution attention—good for rearview mirrors and other tasks that can be done by switching from primary to peripheral attention. Tertiary denotes low resolution—best for small indicator lights and sounds. Sound and movement occupies an ambient awareness at the lowest level of attention.

Soundscapes

Brian Eno coined the term *ambient music* to describes a kind of music meant to influence the mood of the environment without demanding the listener's full attention. When properly designed, sounds can profoundly shape the behaviors of large groups of people, allowing a central actor to quickly communicate something to a large group of people and coordinate them. Music is sometimes pressed into this kind of service. At shopping malls throughout China, "Going Home" by saxophonist Kenny G is played to indicate closing hours. In Taiwan, garbage trucks play a recording of Beethoven's *Für Elise* as a cue for neighborhood residents to bring their garbage out for pickup. Numerous other examples exist on a small scale, but each leverages the same advantages of recorded music: it is specific, recognizable, and unignorable, but also relatively unobtrusive.

The downside, of course, is the risk of a formerly beloved song becoming irritating through constant repetition, creating a negative association with both the song and the event. Anyone who grew up with ice cream trucks playing "It's a Small World" every day of summer is familiar with this phenomenon.

A better solution in these situations is to use generative audio (see the next section) to vary the sound. This provides all the benefits of recognizability and unobtrusiveness, but adds enough variety to avoid irritation.

Generative Audio

Generative audio is a wonderful way to introduce variation and create a constantly evolving sound. This improves human attention. Also called "procedural audio," it is "non-linear...created in real time according to a set of programmatic rules and live input."[9]

You can create generative audio in many different ways:

Linguistic/structural generative audio

Uses generative grammars, like the autocomplete for text messages and Gmail, to form a decision tree that can determine what might come next in a musical piece. Like language, while there are rules for what should come after something else, they are not strict, creating variability. You can create audio with an infinite amount of variability based on the rules given.

Interactive/behavioral generative audio

Doesn't start with inputs, but uses human behavior, such as movement or other interaction with the system, to create music. The system may be previously set up, and interaction from people can

---

9 Andy Farnell, "An Introduction to Procedural Audio and Its Application in Computer Games," *http://cs.au.dk/~dsound/DigitalAudio.dir/Papers/proceduralAudio.pdf.*

modify the music in different ways. For instance, some malls have installation pieces where people can generate music and visuals by walking by at various speeds.

Creative/procedural generative audio
Describes music that is generated by processes that are designed or initiated by the composer. This may mean prerecorded pieces that are combined in particular ways.

Biological/emergent generative audio
Creates music that is infinite and cannot be repeated. An example in nature is the nonrepeating notes created by wind blowing through wind chimes.

Localized Sound

Audio *beamforming* is an advanced way of targeting sound to a specific location, even to the point where someone standing in the targeted area can hear the sound and someone standing two feet away can hear no sound at all. Beamforming works by using an array of speakers and real-time digital signal processing to direct sound to specific areas, while cancelling sound everywhere else. This technique would find a natural application to play audio tracks in an otherwise quiet museum, where patrons can stand in a marked spot and listen to a description of a particular piece of art, or stand outside of it to enjoy the silence. By replacing the need for a handheld audio device, this novel approach would improve hygiene and simplify the experience.

Beamforming can also be used the same way regional temperature control functions in some vehicles, allowing different listeners to control the volume of their experience separately from the other listeners in the room, for instance, for a television. Beamforming works by using an array of speakers and real-time digital signal processing to direct sound to specific areas.

Beamforming could be a big help in hospitals, where patients are often forced to listen to the medical alerts of others and where doctors and nurses experience frequent alert fatigue. What if a nurse could instantly understand the status of a patient just by walking into a room and listening to—instead of looking at—the status of all of the machines?

Alerts could be delivered to contextual, noninterruptive locations in such environments. See Chapter 4 for a detailed discussion of alert fatigue in hospitals.

While beamforming is not a new concept, in the past, it has been expensive in terms of both speakers and computing resources. Improvements in the cost of computing has created affordable signal processing chips which will help bring it to a larger range of applications.

Sound as Therapy

Music therapy has been used in hospitals, schools, and rehabilitation programs, as it has been shown to help some patients struggling with anxiety, depression, and addiction. Sound as therapy has powerful applications, from helping with autism to treating cancer, post-traumatic stress disorder, and Alzheimer's. It can also be safer to use than potentially addictive painkillers, or can be used alongside such medications to reduce their dosage. Sound not only has applications for stress relief and recovery, but it can also help rewire the brain after trauma, overcome speech difficulties, and improve memory.

One example, called NurMut, applies sound to help dementia patients suffering from disorientation, anxiety, and stress. Wearable skin sensors are calibrated to detect the onset of an anxiety attack, using an algorithm that responds to heart rate, movement, and skin conductance. In response to an oncoming attack, the system plays music to calm or cheer the patient.

Sound healing techniques may involve specially tuned singing bowls, singing or chanting, and guided meditation. The singing bowls are often made from machined metal or hand-carved crystal. Their size, shape, and composition allow them to create deep, resonant sound waves in low and high frequencies.

House cats purr at a frequency of 26 Hz, the low end of the 25–250 Hz range produced by felines overall, usually in the key of D, which is known to be soothing. These frequencies promote bone growth and tissue regeneration, leading scientists to hypothesize that cats evolved the purr to stimulate healing while conserving energy and resting. Similar benefits in humans are being investigated: "If scientists were able to mimic the purring of cats, and mechanically stimulate bones and muscles, even when a person was at rest, then the sound [and] vibrations could help induce bone growth, mitigate osteoporosis, and help with muscle loss [and] atrophy in elderly patients or even astronauts in space who face bone density and muscle loss due to weightlessness."[10] One study by NASA using a plate vibrating at 90 Hz found that 10 minutes of therapy per day helped rats maintain near-normal bone density when they were prevented from bearing weight on their hind legs (in comparison, rats who received no treatment lost 92% of normal bone density, and rats that were allowed to bear weight for 10 minutes per day lost 61% of bone density).[11] Studies are currently underway to test similar acoustic therapies on patients with osteoporosis. One day, purring hospital beds could help patients heal.

Conclusion

Sound is an ever-expanding frontier with great depth and surprising applications. There are enormous opportunities to add, reduce, or modify sounds in our environments. By considering sound as a crucial stimulus that can affect our degree of satisfaction, our emotions, and our focus, we can work on designing better sounds that help us instead of work against us.

---

10 "Cat Purring as a Means for Healing Bones," The Infinite Spider, *https://infinitespider. com/cat-purring-and-healing-bones/*.

11 "Good Vibrations," NASA Science, *https://science.nasa.gov/science-news/science-at-nasa/2001/ast02nov_1/*.

Subtractive Sound Design for Products

VEHICLES, BLENDERS, AND HAIR dryers live alongside us in our environments, but they are not always quiet. It's difficult to have a conversation over the sound of a food processor, and an early-morning blow-dry can wake up a housemate. A cheap air conditioning unit or washing machine can also interrupt sleep.

Quiet products have a distinct market advantage. They may be more expensive, and require more research to build, but they are a step forward to products that nonintrusively live alongside us.

This chapter covers how we can learn to make quieter mechanical products, including insights from the automotive industry, the business that has spent the most time and money on "calming down" sound design. Even if you aren't in charge of building a mechanical product, this chapter can help widen your perspective on how much design goes into physical objects with moving parts.

In his 1977 book *The Tuning of the World* (McClelland and Stewart), musician and composer R. Murray Schafer uses the phrase "the flat line sound" to describe the sonic outcome of the Industrial Revolution. The machines that populate the industrialized world, he explains, produce low-information, high-redundancy sounds, and these have largely defined our sonic environment ever since the dawn of industrialization. "In all earlier societies the majority of sounds were discreet and interrupted," he explains, "while today a large portion—perhaps the majority—are continuous."

One aspect of humane sound design begins with an awareness of unenriching sounds and a determination to design around them or eliminate noise when possible. An acoustic camera displays sound as a heatmap, sometimes paired with a video image, as an overlay (Figure

2-1). It creates a highly accurate sound map of the product or environment using measurements made at multiple points. These points can be acquired simultaneously, saving time compared to traditional sound intensity methods. The software allows the calculation of relevant properties of the sound field, such as source strength and direction. From this information it is possible to then create a noise map of the product or location being observed.

FIGURE 2-1

We can hear sound, but we cannot see it. One way to turn the invisible into the visible is to use an acoustic camera, a grid of small microphones that can detect sound and turn it into color. This tool can be extremely helpful in locating the origin of sounds and making them quieter. In this example, you can see the loudest part of the appliance, or the acoustic "hotspot" of the device in red.

Acoustic cameras will likely play a larger role in designing products with sound in the future as the technology becomes more common. They can perform a crucial role in determining where noise comes from, and offer clues about how it might be improved.

English designer James Dyson noticed people complaining about hair dryers being loud, grating, and obtrusive. In response, he spent years developing a revolutionary "quiet" hair dryer. The strategy worked. Customers paid a premium for a more pleasant sonic experience.

You can reduce and even prevent sound by understanding the underlying reasons why it happens in the first place. Most active sound is caused by the movement of components, air, and fluids. By addressing these aspects with better-designed materials and shapes, you can prevent or eliminate sound. When the internal components can't be changed, you can mitigate existing sounds by implementing sound-absorbing materials, containerization, and active and passive sound cancelling. Quieting products requires a combination of attention, marketability, and testing. You can refine things over many design cycles to make them arbitrarily good if you pay attention to the right parameters.

When you calculate the hundreds of hours someone might spend with that product, a quieter product makes sense. Leaf blowers, power tools, and diesel trucks present opportunities for noise reduction. And plenty of products with no moving parts could also benefit from a redesign, such as kitchen sinks, bags of snacks, and the flooring between apartments. There are many strategies for the deliberate design of unnoisy products, but first, we should consider what makes a sound annoying.

What Makes a Sound Annoying?

One tool for measuring the annoyance factor of a sound is called *quasi-peak* detection. This method was originally developed for AM radio in order to detect background interference during broadcast that might interfere with the listening experience. It scans the signal for specific types of sounds: repeating transients, low hums, and other issues. Some methods can then be applied to alter, lessen, or remove the noise in a way that will improve listener satisfaction. Quasi-peak detectors can be built from scratch by using mathematical modeling or noise cancellation, or they can be downloaded as software modules. You can even model them in your head. If you hear the consistent whine of a coil from a bad power supply, you have your own quasi-peak detection. Another measurement is the average power measurement, which adds together and averages the power of the peak waves. Modeling and removing the sound can be done with noise cancellation, software filters, and mechanical designs. This chapter will cover some of these methods.

Frequency and Sound

We are more or less sensitive to sounds based on frequency. By asking subjects to identify when two different frequencies sound equally loud, researchers mapped how sensitive our hearing is across the spectrum (see Figure 2-2).

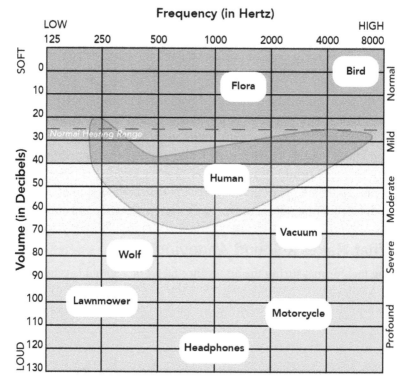

FIGURE 2-2

Frequencies and volume for some common environmental sounds. The chirp of a bird is quiet, but it is at a frequency that can be easily heard, so it does not need to be as loud. The rumble of a truck is low and deep, and something that we both hear and feel.

Our ears are far more sensitive to midrange and high-frequency sounds (see Figure 2-3). Sounds played at high decibel levels in these ranges can harm your ears more easily than slow, low-frequency tones.

Sound at the low end of the spectrum acts like deep waves, and these waves can go through you. You *feel* these sounds more than you hear them. The volume control on your radio accounts for this difference in sensitivity, and actually boosts the bass and treble when the volume is reduced in order to keep a song sounding well balanced.

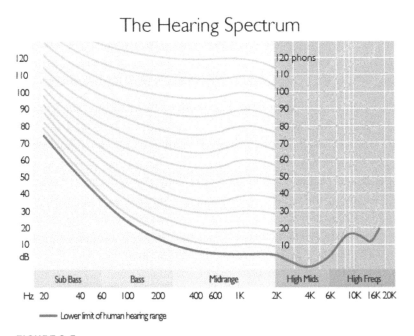

The Hearing Spectrum

FIGURE 2-3

Our ears are more uniformly sensitive to sound at higher decibel levels. We can perceive high-frequency sounds at very low sound-pressure levels of 20 dB. Even though we might feel them, sounds at the sub-bass levels must be at least 70–80 dB before we start to hear them.

To account for how we hear sounds, various weighting standards for sounds have been adopted, such as the dB(A) (or "A-weighting") standard based on the equal loudness curves in Figure 2-2, as well as the B, C, D, and Z standards. Because we hear noise differently than we hear tones, a separate standard was created specifically for noise, called ITU-R 468. This standard is used to accurately capture the severity of noise over an audio signal, such as television or radio broadcasting.

These weighting standards have limitations, however. For instance, although it was created to account for the difference in sensitivity to very quiet sounds where our hearing is more divergent, the dB(A) standard is often pressed into service for applications that it should not be measuring. For example, a number of regulatory agencies have adopted the standard as a requirement for evaluating industrial and environmental noise with respect to the potential for hearing damage and other health effects from sound at all decibel levels, not simply quiet sounds.

Measurements of Loudness

While sound-pressure levels (decibels) are easy to measure, it can be argued that they are less useful for giving us an accurate and intuitive idea of how loud the sound is to us, which is typically what we want.

Phons and sones are units of measurement for the subjective loudness of a sound. Phons are a numerical code for what sounds (as pure tones) are perceived by our hearing as equally loud. Phons can be mathematically converted into sones, as shown in Table 2-1. For tones and other sounds at specific frequencies, sones convey exactly the information presented in the equal loudness curves. Sones also work mathematically the way our ears perceive sound. When you double the measurement of sones, you end up with a sound that is twice as loud, and when you divide it by two, you have a sound half as loud.

TABLE 2-1. A phons-to-sones conversion chart for a tone at 1 kHz. Each frequency requires its own conversion table, which indicates just how complex audio calculations can be. The unit of phons scales with decibels, so every increase of 10 phons—equivalent to a 10 dB increase—results in a doubling of a sound's loudness.

Phon	40	50	60	70	80	90	100	110
Sone	1	2	4	8	16	32	64	128

Thus, sones are a more accurate indicator for the subjective experience of sound because they capture our hearing sensitivity for tones exactly, instead of approximating it through weighting standards. So, if you're making an industrial or motorized product, it can be useful to look at how low frequencies affect people in terms of sones rather than relying entirely on the dB(A) standard.

Judges have even used sones to rule on cases involving noise complaints. The court can hire an audio engineer to calculate the loudness of the sound in sones to reflect what was heard, so that the case accurately represents sound from the human experience, instead of a simple decibel measure.

Some products already carry sound ratings in terms of sones. The quietest certification given by the Home Ventilating Institute is 0.3 sones, which is so quiet that a fan with this rating may need an indicator light to notify the user that it is running. In comparison, a modern refrigerator puts out about 1.0 sones' worth of sound, and the typical bathroom fan is roughly 4.0 sones.

Next we take a look at how these considerations, and other principles of sound, have been applied by manufacturers to quiet their products and improve the user experience.

General Principles for Quiet Products

Cars have improved because companies have iterated a design process to produce components that fit better, lubricants that ease movement between parts, suspension that reduces the transmission of vibrations from the road, and cabins that isolate external noise from the driver. Requirements for noise and pollution levels in the car industry mean that almost every surface of a vehicle is treated, especially in luxury vehicles.

As this section will discuss, we can apply the same general principles of quieting an automobile to quieting other products, although not all aspects will apply to all products.

CREATE GOOD FIT BETWEEN COMPONENTS

A car motor is a complex moving device that must hold together at high speeds. Better-fitting components and quality control improve product quality and product life, reduce rattling and breakage. Along with advances in materials, component fit is a key reason. In the United States in the 1960s and '70s, odometers would count only to 99,999 miles/160,000 km, the expected lifespan of the car. Now, it is common for engines to last twice as long or longer.

Most modern cars require a low-viscosity oil because there simply is no room between the parts to accommodate a thicker oil. If the car does develop wear that loosens the tolerances, the low-viscosity oil can be replaced with a thicker oil that will fill the spaces between the components and enable the engine to continue functioning for many more miles. In other words, instead of remachining the parts for better tolerance, you can just use a thicker oil in it for the next 100,000 miles.

With materials that keep their shape and integrity over time, components can maintain exceptionally tight tolerances almost indefinitely, creating long-lasting products. Engine parts coated with a diamond-like carbon finish show no detectable wear even after 250,000 miles. Companies that identify parts that regularly break can remanufacture those parts from higher-quality materials and save money on repairs and returns.

Creating good fit between components is probably the most expensive option in terms of time and money. It increases development time, equipment tooling, material cost, quality control, and product price. However, when done well, this process can produce high-quality products that can alter an entire industry's verticals. High-quality vacuum cleaner manufacturer Dyson brought in £801 million in 2017, demonstrating that there are business incentives for outstanding design and long-lasting products. Dyson also makes sure that every employee understands the company's core products. "We have every employee on their first day make a vacuum cleaner—even if you're working in customer service," says company founder James Dyson.

Dyson's strength as a company is in uniquely designing everyday products to improve their performance, shape, sound, and function in ways that other companies don't spend enough time considering. The Dyson Supersonic Hair Dryer, which sells for over $400, was designed with a loudness target from the beginning and consequently is the quietest on the market. The Dyson team went through a four-year, $71 million development process. They cut down component size (see Figure 2-4), improved airflow and component fit, and ultimately reduced the sound by 60%. As reported in *Fast Company*, "Getting that tight of a tolerance meant that to hold those pieces together at the right distance while they were being assembled, Dyson had to use stabilizing machines ordinarily used to assemble nuclear weapons," requiring a special license for the machines from the British government.[1]

---

1 Cliff Kuang, "How Dyson Invented a $399 Hairdryer With Nuclear Tech," *Fast Company*, http://bit.ly/2O9O4c8.

FIGURE 2-4
Advertisement for Dyson Supersonic Hair Dryer showing the new machined component (left) compared to a typical hair dryer fan motor. Dyson's approach helped to change a hair dryer market that hadn't been improved in 60 years.

There are products everywhere that can benefit from improved component fit. If you have the time and resources, it is a worthwhile and profitable opportunity. (Dyson is not a publicly traded company, so it can afford to spend money on longer-term design plans instead of defending its quarterly spending.)

Here are some things to consider during the design process:

- Find ways to reduce the number of components.

- Engineer components from a single piece of material.

- Convert components to solid state. (A solid-state hard drive is quieter than a traditional hard drive made from spinning disks and magnets. In addition, solid-state products have fewer opportunities to rattle and fail.)

- Improve material quality to ensure longer life and smoother fit.

- Improve quality control to ensure products can be made consistently.

- When component fit is not perfect, pad materials to insulate against vibration.

- Coat surfaces with advanced vibro-acoustic materials to reduce the bulkiness of designs.

- When applicable, use wet or dry lubricants to help reduce friction and noise in components with hard surfaces.

MINIMIZE UNOCCUPIED SPACE

Car bodies with empty space act like resonance chambers to increase the intensity of unwanted sounds. When automobile manufacturers can't remove empty space through design, engineers will fill it with sound-absorbing materials and custom foam inserts.

In this era of product design, smaller, more streamlined products are more successful. Creating a product with little unused space and a uniform distribution of weight can be a mark of quality. Apple is notorious for the closely fitting components in MacBooks and iPhones, making those products slimmer and quieter. Resonance cavities make sense if you're trying to create a specific acoustic experience, but this must be an intentional product choice. Removing unwanted space might be more expensive, but this process can create products that last longer and sound better. As with setting an acoustic target at the beginning of the design process, challenge your designers and engineers to come up with creative ways to remove unused space in their designs.

ADD SOUND-ABSORBING MATERIALS

When component fit is not perfect or there are unavoidable empty spaces inside products, sound-absorbing materials can help by insulating parts of the product from other pieces, absorbing vibrations, and protecting components. A sound-absorbing material is anything that weakens sound waves. In automobiles, sound-absorbing materials can typically be easily removed, replaced, or enhanced.

Cars have sound-absorbing materials behind virtually every panel. Metal doors are especially prone to vibration, so most vehicles have loose batting or foam padding inside the car door (see Figure 2-5). It is common to find acoustic materials under the hood and in the trunk. Luxury vehicles use the highest-quality materials, and can contain more than 100 pounds (45 kilograms) of materials to help quiet the ride. For cheaper vehicles, aftermarket DIY kits with precut sound-absorbing panels are widely available for many models on the market.

FIGURE 2-5

Different acoustic materials used inside of a common car door. A piece of foam keeps the steel doorplate from wobbling during travel, and cloth baffling absorbs extra vibrations.

The same principles of sound absorption can be used in a variety of other products, from small kitchen-sized devices to microscopic materials.

Advances in materials science have allowed us to do more with less bulk, and there is an opportunity in the world of consumer electronics for the development of new dense materials to better isolate sound in and around electronic components. Ideally, such a material could be injected into electronic devices, much like spray foam is added to walls for insulation in buildings. Such a material could protect components and provide a more pleasant acoustic experience. Current materials trade off between heat insulation and acoustic dampening—to dissipate heat you need a conductor, but if you want to dampen sound, you need a dense material like a polymer, which ends up being an insulator of heat. A new material composite could theoretically have both properties. The ideal composite would be *viscoelastic*: somewhat stretchy and soft, and capable of bouncing back to its original shape when deformed.

It would need to have a relatively high density to prevent sound vibrations, and could be blended with a material such as a resin, carbide, fiberglass, or plastic composite to give it some structure.

If you have the budget, consider researching recent advances in new materials science. There may be cheaper, lighter, and easier-to-use products that can give you the acoustic effects you're looking for.

ADD SURFACE TREATMENTS

A surface treatment can change the acoustic properties of noisy materials, such as sheet metal or steel inside a car door, making it sound completely different.

Cars contain plastic, metal, glass, foam, rubber, cloth, vinyl, and other materials. Each material can respond differently on the road or to the effects of air and liquid turbulence. You're likely to find a mixture of rubberized asphalt (see Figure 2-6) in the wheel wells and on the undercarriage to absorb vibration from tires and road noise.

European manufacturers keep car cabins quiet by coating car doors with metal-infused vinyl. This surface treatment is also used by the car audio industry to make a better environment for car stereos. Cheaper cars skip acoustic treatments, opening up the market for DIY solutions such as polyurethane sound-deadening paints for metal panels.

High-end electronics add polymer coatings to aluminum casings to improve their feel and acoustic properties. Tablet stands include a layer of silicon material to deaden sound when they're placed on a table. Blenders and other motorized household appliances have silicon or rubber bases.

Many products could benefit from surface treatments. It is worthwhile to consider design scenarios for unexpected objects. We all know that sinks are loud—they reflect the sound of dishes clinking and water turbulence. What materials could be used to make a sink quieter? Could a sink benefit from a surface treatment that would adhere and last? What about quieter plates or silverware? There are so many opportunities to make products better in ways that are important to sensitive humans. There are sounds in our environment that we don't need; consider ways to remove them, even if they seem absurd. A quiet bowling pin? Why not?!

FIGURE 2-6

A surface treatment, rubberized asphalt, used in the trunk of a car to reduce rattling.

ADD CONTAINERS TO COMPONENTS OR AROUND PRODUCTS

Containers trap sound by preventing it from exiting or entering a space. This is why engine noise is quieter in a car cabin. Casings are one of the easiest ways to reduce sound. If there is a component that can be isolated and encased, there is no specialized math that needs to be done, provided the casing does not accidentally act as its own resonance chamber. Gaps must be eliminated because they transmit sound more easily. DIY car soundproofing sites prioritize sealing all air gaps in the car cabin prior to making other modifications.

Blendtec and Vitamix use nesting casings to make some of the quietest (and most expensive) blenders in the world, and Amazon advertises aftermarket container solutions that can be placed over any blender to reduce noise. This container-within-a-container method can trap sounds at multiple levels, resulting in a product that has less vibration, sound, and overall intrusiveness. Containers can help quiet many motorized products and should be considered during the design process.

ADD HELMHOLTZ CAVITIES

A Helmholtz cavity is a more advanced form of antivibration technology that creates a resonance chamber to cancel sound vibration destructively. Mufflers use Helmholtz cavities to capture sound waves and reflect each wave perfectly out of phase with itself, neutralizing its energy (Figure 2-7). These cavities can greatly reduce the amount of sound produced by an engine, leaving a dramatically quieter result.

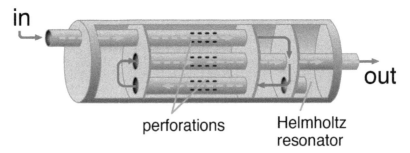

FIGURE 2-7
A Helmholtz cavity in a car's muffler.

Though they are not useful in products that need wide-spectrum cancellation, Helmholtz cavities are a good solution for very loud or annoying sounds that fall within a narrow spectrum. You can even tune them to cancel specific acoustic frequencies of your choosing within that narrow range. Dyson was innovative in using Helmholtz cavities to reduce the characteristic high-pitched whine of its hair dryers. This produced a more expensive but also more pleasant and more sought-after product with a unique sonic profile. There are other types of reactive silencing methods that use resonances to cancel acoustic frequencies, but the Helmholtz cavity is a good starting point to explore during the design process. They can be any shape and are designed for a specific frequency using a simple equation that will dictate the cavity's volume and neck diameter.

ISOLATE VIBRATION OF MOVING PARTS SO THE VIBRATION IS NOT TRANSMITTED

A car's suspension isolates the engine vibrations from the rest of the vehicle, including the car's body. This results in a smoother, quieter ride for passengers. There are even special ways to engineer tire treads to further isolate sound.

You might remember the egg drop competition from your school's science class. The goal was to put an egg in a container and drop it from the top of a building without cracking the egg. If you are familiar with this challenge, you have probably seen a design suspending the egg inside a nested container with rubber bands or another elastic medium. The outside of the container may experience a rough ride, but hopefully enough of the movement is isolated from the egg that it reaches the ground safely. This technique can be applied to many products to both reduce overall sound and insulate fragile elements from damage.

One of the easiest ways to quiet a blender is to set it on a rubberized pad on the countertop. The rubberized pad will absorb some of the vibration and quiet the product. It's a good practice to always place motors and other vibrating components on a rubberized base. This small change can greatly impact the sound of a product.

Many new apartment buildings are made from concrete, reducing the sound that travels between units. But older apartment buildings, especially those with in-unit washers and dryers, suffer from noise insulation issues. Individual washers and dryers can send vibrations into the ceilings of the apartments below them, and multiple machines running simultaneously can add a layer of noise to the entire structure. To solve this, many apartment buildings in Berlin utilize 2–3 cm antivibration mats underneath each machine to isolate mechanical vibrations from the ceilings of the apartments below.

Placing elastic materials between panels can also have a quieting effect. Some types of polymer coatings can provide enough cushioning between the individual parts of a product case to prevent sound, while adding only minimal cost, weight, and bulk.

Active vibration cancellation and noise cancellation

All sound is waves. The images in Figure 2-8 show waves in water—the kind of waves we are most accustomed to seeing. They are a good place to begin to visualize sound. Water waves are typically a form of transverse wave (with a small amount of compression between molecules), so individual molecules of water move up and down as the wave passes. Sound, in contrast, is fully a compression wave, so the individual molecules of air (or in a liquid or solid, depending on the medium) grow closer together and then farther apart as the wave passes.

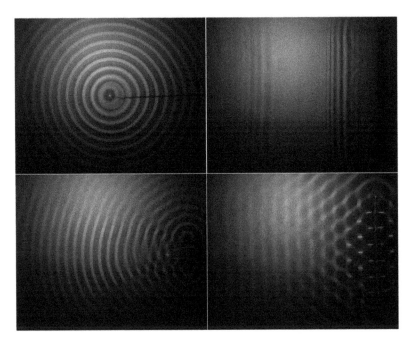

FIGURE 2-8

Electric motors convert the signal to generate the waves in the water shown in this series of images. Light refracts differently in the troughs and the peaks of the waves, rendering the waves visible. Top left: waves in all directions, uninterrupted by walls. Top right: A wave source reflecting back from a wall. Bottom left: Two wave sources with destructive interference. Bottom right: Multiple circular waves producing additive interference. The light points are where the waves pile up in higher energies.

Water waves and sound waves possess the same kinds of interference patterns shown in Figure 2-8, reflecting against surfaces and dissipating when the waves lose energy.

Two identical waveforms can double in power when added; or, when played out of phase, they can actually cancel each other out (see Figure 2-9). Two waves added together in phase—where the peaks of one wave line up with the peaks on the other—results in a louder, amplified sound. This is called *constructive interference*. Waves that are out of phase—when the peaks of one wave line up with the troughs of another—behave differently. The peaks will cancel out the troughs, either silencing or reducing the overall sound. This is called *destructive interference*.

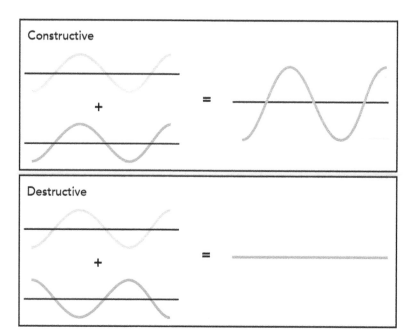

FIGURE 2-9

Two of the same sounds can add up to create a louder sound, or, when played out of phase with each other, can eliminate the sound entirely.

Noise-cancelling headphones work because they have two components: a microphone that detects sound and a speaker that plays the inverse wave, cancelling the sound. GM used active noise cancellation in recent vehicles to improve fuel efficiency.[2] By cancelling a particular disruptive low-frequency sound, GM can run the engines at their most efficient RPM range, which otherwise is avoided because of the noise.

Active vibration cancellation works on the same principle as noise cancellation, but the vibrations are cancelled at the mechanical stage. Mechanical vibration is measured and cancelled through destructive interference by producing the opposite vibration of the one that needs to be removed.

Active vibration cancellation is such a powerful method for absorbing unwanted movement that it is used in the foundations of tall buildings to reduce rattling and destruction during earthquakes. As reported in the *Washington Post*, "The most sophisticated systems employ fluid-filled

2 Darren Quick, "GM Uses Active Noise Cancellation Technology to Improve Fuel Economy," *http://bit.ly/2CMX8l3*.

shock absorbers that slosh thick oil in the opposite direction of any swaying. One of the tallest buildings in Tokyo, the 781-foot Roppongi Hills Mori Tower, included such a 'semi-active oil damper' design when completed in 2003."[3]

One patent by Google accomplishes the same vibration cancelling on a smaller scale using magnetic levitation, and other devices create direct opposing mechanical vibration. We can do the same for our products by using mechanical vibration cancellation or other means. The principles of vibration-cancelling systems could be miniaturized and made inexpensive through development and iteration.

Some companies have attempted to use mechanical vibration to turn surfaces such as windows into noise-cancelling speakers. In the late 2010s, Muzo and Sono created products that could be placed on a window to block noise from the outside world. Sono reported cancellations of up to 12 dB from outside noise, but the product could not block out the entire spectrum of low- and high-frequency sounds. Road and construction noise could still be heard through the windows. This area is rife with opportunity, as more and more people live in busy cities with increased traffic. Some proposed designs for windows instead use Helmholtz cavities.

Masking Unwanted Sounds with Other Noises

If you can't remove noise, you could play another noise to mask it (Figure 2-10). You can easily find pink and white noise sources online, and can listen through speakers or headphones to cover up unwanted sounds that cannot be easily tuned out.

Masking sounds come in different "colors." In the visible spectrum, the longest wavelengths of light are red and the shortest wavelengths are blue or violet. Likewise, to emphasize higher or lower frequencies, the sound spectrum also uses the color analogy, even though sound waves are not actually visible.

---

3 Brian Vastag, "Japan a Leader in Engineering Earthquake-Proof Structures, Helping Limit Damage," *Washington Post*, https://wapo.st/2F8gaoK.

The basic noise distribution is referred to as *white noise*, because, like white light, it represents all frequencies equally. One example of white noise is the sharp and hissy sound of television static. White noise works to drown out other background interruptions because it plays sound across all frequencies, so it is likelier to mask a variety of unwanted, interruptive sounds. However, low frequencies may still be perceptible.

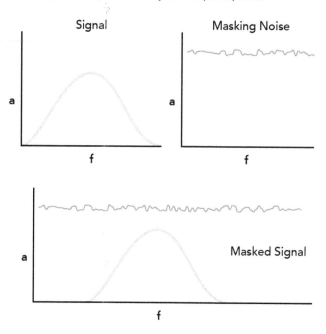

FIGURE 2-10

How a masking sound works. Playing noise covers up unwanted signals and prevents annoyances.

Pink noise shifts from white noise toward lower frequencies with longer wavelengths, making it slightly deeper, smoother, and less intense. It sounds more like being next to a waterfall, so it can help mask lower-frequency sounds. Red noise emphasizes low frequencies even more than pink, and brown noise emphasizes the lower frequencies so much that it emulates the sound of thunder or the distant roar of a very large waterfall. It is even more likely to mask low frequencies entering a space.

In contrast, blue noise emphasizes higher frequencies. While it might not be as calming as the other colors, it could be used to cover up sharp, high-frequency sounds.

REDUCE TURBULENCE OF AIR AND FLUID MOVEMENT

Turbulence from air or fluid moving over or around a surface generates noise. We can reduce this noise by smoothing the flow.

Exterior shape

Cars have been optimized to streamline the movement of air. The shape of a car affects its speed and performance. An elongated teardrop, like the cross-section of an airplane wing, is a fundamentally aerodynamic shape (Figure 2-11). The more car exteriors emulated this shape, the more streamlined the cars became (Figure 2-12).

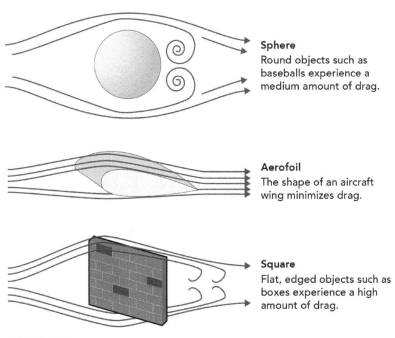

Sphere
Round objects such as baseballs experience a medium amount of drag.

Aerofoil
The shape of an aircraft wing minimizes drag.

Square
Flat, edged objects such as boxes experience a high amount of drag.

FIGURE 2-11
Fluid and airflow around various object shapes.

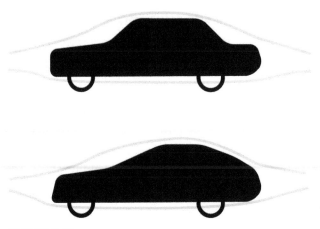

FIGURE 2-12
Streamlined vehicle designs prevent eddies created by airflow

Shape and materials

One of the most important parts of vehicle efficiency is how the exhaust leaves the car. An exhaust manifold combines many flows exiting the combustion chambers into one single flow and conducts hot gases away from the engine. The shape of an exhaust manifold is just as important as the material it is made from. Many manifolds are made from cast iron (Figure 2-13), as they are less prone to breaking, but titanium manifolds increase vehicle efficiency because they are smoother on the inside than cast iron. This results in fewer eddies in the hot air that passes through it, decreasing turbulence. However, titanium must be welded together, and is prone to breakage at these welds. The most advanced exhaust manifolds are made from 3D-printed titanium. This requires no welding and ensures a smooth, uniform overall shape.

FIGURE 2-13
Cast-iron exhaust manifold

Airflow through products

Stationary products, like fans, will have air moving through them. It's important to regulate their input and output. Simple modifications can reduce turbulence.

You can achieve orderly airflow by using passageways with smooth, nontextured surfaces and eliminating sharp turns or corners in favor of gentle turns (see Figure 2-14). Many product designers cool product components by placing them in the path of the moving air. Use an elongated teardrop shape, rather than a boxy exterior, to cover components that require cooling in order to reduce noise and inefficiencies.

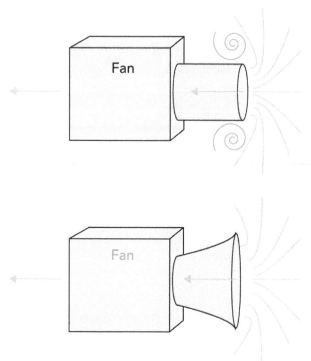

FIGURE 2-14
Airflow intake and output in a fan. A sharp intake (top) will create eddies that cause sound and reduce efficiencies. A fluted intake (bottom) will smooth incoming air and improve product performance.

A wealth of research exists on optimizing the shape of fan blades, both for consumer and industrial products. Large ducts can reduce air speed, leading to quieter flow. When slowing the airflow is not an option, smooth airflow is necessary.

Liquid flow through products

Many of the principles for creating smooth airflow can also be applied to liquids, although there are some exceptions. Slow-moving fluid is quieter than fast-moving fluid. Smooth surfaces and curves are quieter than textured surfaces and sharp turns. Fluids also are special cases because they are denser than air. This density can lead to problems with pressure waves as fluids flow through products. Some of the solutions for liquids diffuse these pressure waves by passing them through "leaky tubes" to improve flow.

There are multiple solutions to the problem of quieting fluids and fluid flow through vehicle parts. The automotive industry has applied advanced techniques to reduce the noise associated with the flow of power steering fluid, for example. Adding a section of hose, restrictors, or a coaxial tuning cable with hose are all solutions used to reduce the amplitude of pressure waves, likely using the principle of destructive interference.[4]

Laminar flow

You've probably seen laminar flow in pour spouts used in cocktail bars or olive oil bottles (see Figure 2-15). A laminar pour spout creates a nonturbulent liquid flow by aligning the liquid molecules' pathways so that they run in parallel and do not interfere with each other. This creates a pleasant pouring experience because there is no liquid resistance—the equivalent of reducing air drag. Applied industrially, laminar flow reduces noise and disorder within functional products, eliminating energy loss.

FIGURE 2-15

An example of a bottle nozzle with laminar flow. The nozzle directs the flow of liquid into a smooth, nonturbulent pour.

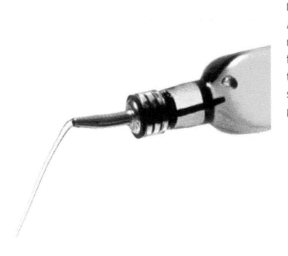

---

4   Chuan-Chiang Chen, Olakunle Harrison, and Adrian K. McKinney, "Investigation of Fluidborne Noise Reduction in Automotive Hydraulic Power Steering Systems," *Journal of Applied Mechanical Engineering* 1, no. 110 (2012), *http://bit.ly/2O9rAbg.*

Conclusion

Removing unenriching sound is one of the greatest frontiers in new product design. It is worth taking the time to explore creative solutions that incorporate new or previously unconsidered materials and techniques. We can learn from industries that have spent billions on designing objects that work well for years, under a variety of conditions. The opportunity to make profitable products with sound reduction is enormous. With a dedicated consideration of their construction, many overlooked everyday objects could become bestsellers.

Adding Sound to Interactions

A Brief History of Sound Design

THE HISTORY OF HUMAN civilization is also a history of increasingly complex sound design. As humans gathered into larger groups and more permanent settlements, sounds were refined to be louder, more distinctive, and more customized.

Originating in West Africa, the talking drum was an early, elegant solution to the very common problem of communicating over a distance. Without consonants and vowels, the drums mimicked the rhythm and pitch of common poetic phrases that could be translated into known meanings. Much like how the alphabet song can be recognized when hummed, the phrases had a rhythm and set of tones that could be identified in a tonal drum beat. The talking drum communicated simple messages—the date of a ceremony or warning of an attack, for example—with other drums picking up signals and repeating them further along.

The amount of detail that could be conveyed was considerably lower than that of human speech, but much higher than the binary "on/off" conveyed by an alarm. It turns out that many group-level communication tasks fit neatly into this format. Although not the first device to convey variable messages at a distance, the talking drum was far more versatile than any other auditory communication device of its day. It was unique because of its combination of flexibility, resolution, and range.

Since then, humans have developed ever more sophisticated ways to convey messages over a distance, and a good fraction of them involve sound. Our first progression into electrically enabled long-distance communication was Morse code. It employed sound, and enabled communication that has proved extremely useful for large groups like militaries, businesses, and governments.

Today, the variety of communication media we employ is astoundingly rich. Even in an era when millions have the ability to quickly record and send high resolution videos, we often resort to brief text messages, or willingly submit ourselves to Twitter's 280-character limit. There is a certain wisdom to this. Whether in sound, text, or image, a limited amount of information is often preferable, especially when we are asked to absorb thousands of such messages in a day.

Audio communication has evolved from tribal messages sent over short distances to true long-distance communication. The advent of radio scaled the ability to communicate enormously; it allowed for transmission of news as well as music and emergency messages. Far from passing information between small tribes of hundreds of people, new methods of communication enabled thousands, then millions, and now billions of citizens to keep in touch through audio across the world.

Now we hear thousands of sounds each day, almost without realizing it, from car horns and police sirens, school bells and smartphone alerts, to microwave beeps and fire alarms. The increasing density of cities has created larger arenas for noise pollution.

SOUND AND PRODUCTS

There is no such thing as an entirely digital product. Even though a sound might be created on a computer, all sound is translated through the mechanical speakers that it's played back on. Every sound wave in the world comes out of physicality. The quality of hardware creates the difference between the shrill beep of a microwave and the range of sounds produced by movie theater speakers. Once the sound waves begin, they are also reflected back or absorbed by their environment. The environment affects how we perceive the sound. Buildings, trees, cars, and mountains influence how a sound is perceived. Even changes in humidity can affect how sound waves reach us and how we perceive them.

Some objects indicate their behavior and status through the materials from which they are made. Consider a baseball bat hitting a baseball, or an axe successfully splitting a piece of wood. Both produce sounds that give a lot of information about the action performed, and about the qualities of the objects themselves, but neither has been explicitly "sound-designed." Still other products benefit from the tuning of their "passive" acoustic characteristics: weights are added to car doors in order to make them feel more solid when they are opened and produce a sturdy *crumpf* sound when they are closed.

As designers, we can affect how a product or experience sounds by changing materials, speaker hardware, and the digital audio file that's played on the hardware. These different levels of design are important to keep in mind as we consider when to add sound (the subject of this chapter) or remove sound (the subject of Chapter 4) from products or interactions.

Sound travels through the air, and air envelops us like water surrounds a fish. It is always there, and it is something we cannot opt out of experiencing. This should remind designers that we may be adding to an already-overloaded channel. Adding sounds should aim to improve the user experience, augment a display, or enhance an environment. "Do I need to add sound here?" should be the first question you ask before jumping in and specifying or designing sound for a product.

Types of Notifications

We expect feedback from our interactions. The majority of actions in the natural world produce sounds. Just as we hear a stone when we drop it into a lake and see the ripples on the water, we must engineer a sound when we interact with a digital product. We've carried some sounds from the analog world to the digital one; for example, digital cameras use shutter sounds that have been re-created and added to make them sound like their analog ancestors. This is an example of *auditory skeuomorphism*, which is discussed in the section, "Take Cues from the Natural World."

Audio notifications convey status, feedback, and instructions. Some sounds come from the products themselves, such as mechanical sounds. Other sounds give us necessary feedback, such as an incorrect password attempt. Some sounds are informational, such as driving directions or backing-up alerts on trucks, or indicate status, such as a low battery alert or fire alarm. And still other sounds are unnecessary and interfere with our senses; we can remove them using principles of subtractive audio design.

The following are examples of notification sounds organized by type:

Mechanical

- Shutter on an analog camera
- Sewing machine when it starts stitching
- Vehicle motor as revolutions per minute (RPMs) increase
- Tires of a car on the road
- Toast popping up out of a toaster
- Sprinklers turning on

Feedback

- Keypresses on a mobile phone
- Keycard success in a hotel room lock
- Keycard failure
- Password incorrect
- Remove your credit card from the chip reader
- Shutter on a digital camera
- Buttons on a keypad
- Keys on a keyboard
- Device is recording

Informational

- Driving directions
- Seatbelt reminder
- A vehicle is backing up—stay away

Status alerts

- This device has low power
- Text message received
- The water has boiled
- Smoke in the room detected
- It is okay to cross the street

- The food is done

- An appointment is coming up

A few of the notifications listed here, such as keypresses or "this device is recording" can also be accomplished through visual-only or haptic-only approaches. Once you determine the type of notification your product needs, you can decide whether it should have an audio component or not.

When to Add Audio Notifications

The following list may be helpful in deciding when sound may be preferable to a visual notification:

The message is simple and short.

Communicating a brief piece of information often makes more sense as an audio alert, especially if the user's attention is elsewhere.

- Tiny tone or double-haptic tap: *You have received a text message.*

- Repeating haptic percussion or short tone: *Someone is calling you.*

The message refers to events in time.

Similar to the preceding item, you should choose audio alerts when you need a time-based notification during a task where the user can't be expected to hang around watching the clock.

- Repeated tone or chime: *The cake has finished baking.*

The message won't be referenced again later.

Sound makes sense when there's no need for a record—for example, scanning a badge in order to unlock a door. In a situation like this, a simple beep confirms success without requiring the user to look down.

- Small green light and minimal clack: *Access granted.*

Information is continuously changing.

The sound of a car engine creates automatic, mechanical feedback for the motor's RPM, telling the driver when it is a good time to shift without adding clutter to the visual UI. When the sound is not produced mechanically—for instance, in an electric vehicle—that mechanical, variable information is lost. Sonification could replace the loss of information using real-time data of the vehicle's RPMs or speed.

- ○ Revving sound that increases with engine's RPM: *The engine is at 3,500 RPM, and rising.*
- ○ Sonic "ticks" that track when a Geiger counter detects increasing levels of radiation: *Radiation levels are increasing.*

The user's eyes are focused elsewhere.

The most obvious and pressing reason for using audio is when it would be inconvenient or dangerous for the user to look at a visual indicator. Many automotive navigation systems are equipped with a voice interface for this very reason.

- ○ Spoken voice: *In 100 meters, turn left.*

The environment limits visibility, or the user is visually impaired.

When a visual interface is likely to be obscured, or when designing for the visually impaired, use auditory confirmations to augment visual indicators.

- ○ A discrete, repeating high-pitched sound such as the synthetic bird-chirping sound emitted by a walk signal: *It is now safe to cross the street.*

The recipient is moving or out of visual range.

Sound is usually mandatory for emergency warnings because it doesn't require the user to be looking in any particular direction when the message is delivered, while bright back-up lights indicate danger to those who cannot hear.

- ○ Sharp, high-pitched, screeching tone with additional flashing lights: *There's a fire somewhere in this building!*

The user needs to be informed of a complex set of information.

In some cases, a sound element needs to carry more complex information. In these situations, it may be useful to use a *two-stage signal.*

Airport announcements, in which a tone or short melody acts as a primer and is followed by a voice announcement, are one example. The first stage of the signal can alert the user that a complex piece of information is about to be delivered. Another example is the "ready-action" couplet in certain pieces of wireless audio equipment, such as Bluetooth speakers. An initial tone indicates readiness for pairing, and a second, usually more complex signal indicates that pairing has been successful. Using this two-stage approach makes it easier for the user to troubleshoot problems without having to add a display or force the user to approach the device.

- Tone—1-second pause—announcement: *Will passenger Carlos Miranda please come to the Lufthansa ticket desk?*

Guidelines for Adding Sounds to Interactions

It is important to consider what kinds of situations and sound types might best fit each kind of interaction. In this section we'll describe a list of guidelines for adding sound.

TAKE CUES FROM THE NATURAL WORLD

Electronic devices take cues from the natural and mechanical worlds for inspiration in sound design. This is why your smartphone makes a subtle mechanical click when you unlock it. Designers debated whether camera apps should go entirely *skeuomorphic* (using an element in a digital user interface to mimic a physical object—in this case, a recording of a real camera shutter) or entirely digital (an artificial beep), but the sweet spot in this case turned out to be somewhere in the middle, with a slightly pared-down version of the shutter sound. Human brains, it seems, like sounds that are familiar but not too familiar. Engine sounds, from the rev of the motor to the exhaust manifold, are often tuned to sound larger and more intense than they really are. We expect cars to sound a certain way, and we have a collective memory of early models and the sounds they created. Sound designers tune motor sounds specifically to work with those expectations.

CONSIDER NOTIFICATION LENGTH

The more often an alert or notification occurs, the shorter and less intense it should be (Figure 3-1). Conversely, if something happens at longer, irregular intervals, such as a phone call, the sound should be a bit longer and more intense.

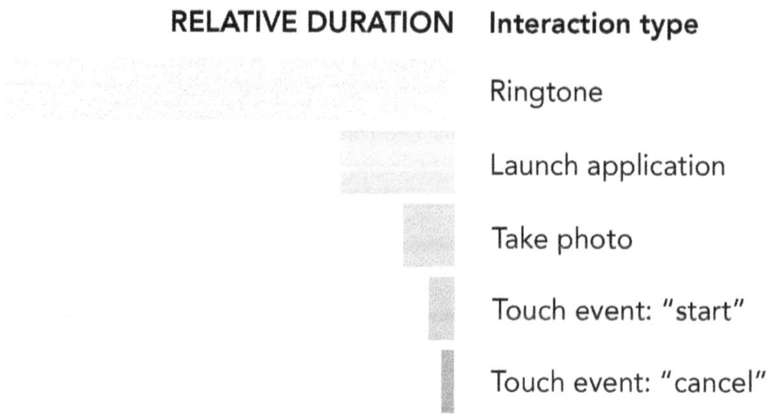

RELATIVE DURATION	Interaction type
	Ringtone
	Launch application
	Take photo
	Touch event: "start"
	Touch event: "cancel"

FIGURE 3-1
Sounds that you hear often, such as navigation feedback or typing, should be short.

Chat notification sounds are a good example of feedback that should be as quiet and short as possible.

DETERMINE NOTIFICATION CONTEXT

Consider "nonuse" cases for sound notifications. How can you design notifications so they are played only when needed and useful?

Most washers and dryers have a sound to announce when they are done with a load. During the day, this is useful and allows the user to switch a load or take it out to fold. But when the user starts a cycle at night before going to bed, it can become a nuisance.

What makes sense in the user-experience testing lab under optimal conditions often does not make sense in the real world.

Consider time of day or activity. Do you want to play a loud sound after dark? Would you want to interrupt someone while they are driving? While they are running a music app? Ensuring the product is tested in a variety of circumstances, inconvenient or not, can prevent a lot of incorrect assumptions.

CONSIDER VOLUME

The decibel is the objective measurement of sound. It simply measures the pressure level above resting air. The physical measurement of sound is different from our *subjective* perception of sound. Although sound doubles its physical energy every 3 decibels, when translated into the subjective experience of how loudness is perceived, a sound doubles in loudness approximately every 10 decibels.

The ear perceives the volume of different frequencies differently. We also perceive complex sounds as louder than simple ones. This is because the brain sums multiple frequencies in complex sounds and the overall stimulation of our auditory nerves to arrive at our subjective perception of sound. A greater number of auditory nerves firing contributes to a greater sense of loudness. For a similar reason, but in the opposite direction, sounds of very short duration (fractions of a second) sound less loud than sounds of longer duration. Very short sounds don't sound like tones at all to us, but instead are perceived as "clicks" that are either bright or dull depending on the frequency of sound that made them (the higher the sound, the "brighter" the click).

The frequency of the sound also makes a difference. Some sounds are barely audible at 50 dB, while others are quite distinct. A quiet conversation measures about 50 dB and is mostly composed of upper bass and midrange frequencies, the range of the human voice.

As shown in Figure 3-2, a library is typically half as loud as a quiet conversation, while rustling leaves, about the volume of a whisper, are eight times quieter. A garbage disposal is eight times as loud as a quiet conversation, but a jackhammer is four times louder than that.

1024x	150dB	Jet takeoff
512x	140dB	Aircraft carrier deck
256x	130dB	Military jet takeoff
128x	120dB	Thunderclap
64x	110dB	Rock concert
32x	100dB	Jackhammer
16x	90dB	Motorcycle at 25 feet
8x	80dB	Garbage disposal
4x	70dB	Vacuum cleaner
2x	60dB	Restaurant conversation
1x	**50dB**	**Quiet conversation**
1/2x	40dB	Library
1/4x	30dB	Quiet rural area
1/8x	20dB	Whisper
1/16x	10dB	Normal breathing

FIGURE 3-2

Relative loudness of different sounds. The level of a quiet conversation is an arbitrary but important human reference point for comparison.

The need for volume decreases the closer you expect the user to be to the product when the sound is played. Consider the average distance you expect the user to be from the device and reduce the volume for close interactions. Also consider the context when setting the default volume of the product and allow the user to easily set or change it. Being able to change the sound of the washer in your small apartment is preferable to being stuck with a sound that is too loud.

When notifications need to be heard from another room, the volume can be higher and customized to transmit well through walls while still being identifiable (through rhythm or tone color) after losing some high-frequency content.

If a sound is subtle enough, it can just tickle the edge of your subconscious without overburdening your primary channel of attention (Figure 3-3).

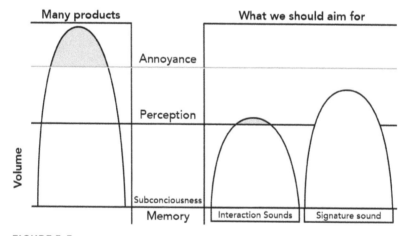

FIGURE 3-3

Aiming for brand or auditory recognition just above the subconscious level is one way to ensure a sound will feel natural to users.

It is possible for a phone to "sniff" its environment before sounding a notification, and to adjust its volume depending on whether it is in an enclosed environment. The phone plays a short burst of sound at around 19 kHz, a frequency outside the hearing range that is easily masked by background noise, and then "listens" for any reverberation. If it hears reverb, then the phone senses it is in an open space and likely needn't play a sound loudly to get attention. On the other hand, if there is no reverb, the phone senses it is in a bag or other enclosed space and adjusts its volume accordingly.

It is also possible for a device to sample the ambient noise and adjust the volume or convert the notification to haptic if the environment is very loud.

Make sure to balance the volume of multiple sounds. Imagine a song where each instrument was set to its maximum loudness regardless of how it sounded in relation to the others. Adjusting the volume of different sounds relative to each other, and in light of their function, is important for creating a good user experience.

DESIGN SOUND FOR HOW IT WILL INTERACT WITH OBJECTS

The wavelength of a sound affects how it interacts with a space. In general, the lower the frequency, the more it tends to spread in all directions. Lower frequencies tend to go through solids, while higher frequencies act more like rays and tend to stop when they hit something solid (see Figure 3-4).

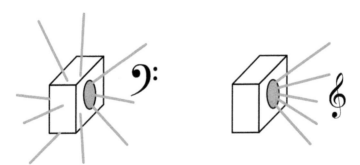

FIGURE 3-4
How sounds play through a speaker. From the speaker on the left, bass travels through the speaker cabinet; the higher the treble frequencies, the more a speaker behaves like a spotlight.

This is important to keep in mind while you're adding sounds. If your product produces a sound inside a bag or in a room down the hall, the high-frequency content of the sound may be lost by the time it reaches a listener, simply because of the way sound interacts with objects. Test your sounds with the high-frequency content filtered out to see how they will sound in these contexts.

CONSIDER THE FREQUENCY OF THE SOUND

Whether a sound is irritating or pleasing has as much to do with frequency as it does loudness and quality. Many things can affect the way a given sound is perceived.

A 2012 study in the *Journal of Neuroscience* used a functional MRI (which displays real-time images of activity in the brain) to study the brain's response to 74 different sounds.[1] The study found that annoying sounds triggered "highly emotional response[s] in the brain," and that the most emotionally triggering sounds were in a specific frequency range. The most unpleasant sounds, ranging from chalk screeching on a chalkboard to a baby's scream, were located in the higher frequency range of 2,000 to 5,000 Hz. This primitive reaction was categorized as a "possible distress signal from the amygdala to the auditory cortex." The most pleasing sounds were found to be running water, applause, and babies laughing, sounds we associate with intrinsically positive emotions.

The left sides of Figures 3-5 and 3-6 contain sub-bass and bass frequencies. Sounds in these frequency ranges are more difficult to hear at low levels, but they can be felt. One of the reasons we feel bass frequencies is because they resonate in our chest and throat. Just listen to a car blasting music as it drives down the street. You probably can't hear the higher notes in the music, but you can hear and feel the low-frequency *boom boom boom* as it rolls by you. Figure 3-7 shows the frequency of several musical instruments.

---

1   Sukhbinder Kumar, Katharina von Kriegstein, Karl Friston, and Timothy D. Griffiths, "Features Versus Feelings: Dissociable Representations of the Acoustic Features and Valence of Aversive Sounds," *Journal of Neuroscience* 32, no. 41 (2012): 14184–14192, http://www.jneurosci.org/content/32/41/14184.

The Hearing Spectrum

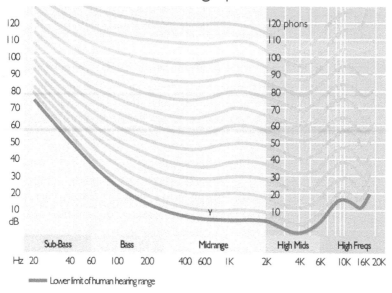

Lower limit of human hearing range

FIGURE 3-5

The hearing spectrum. High mids, in the region where the brain is most sensitive to sound, do not need to be very loud for us to detect them.

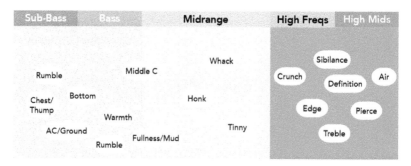

FIGURE 3-6

Some descriptive words for various sounds on the frequency spectrum.

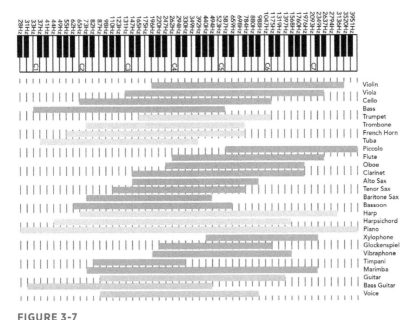

FIGURE 3-7

The frequency graph of various instruments.

Bass and midrange can give sound some fullness, but toward the high-mid range, we get some tinniness to the sounds. Mid-frequency and high-frequency coincide with the range of the human voice in spoken communication, so we are particularly attuned to this range. Sounds in the high-mid frequency range can be annoying or even painful to us before they reach the same level of energy as other sounds. This is because our ears are the most sensitive to sounds in this range.

We get piercing sounds toward the high frequencies. Fire alarms usually consist of loud, shrill sounds, and it is the frequency as much as the loudness that creates this effect. Fire alarm sounds are in the high-frequency range for a reason. These frequencies sit in what are called *critical bands*: the range of frequencies that the human ear is most sensitive to. The archetypical annoying beep sits between 2,000 and 4,000 Hz: it is the frequency range we are most likely to hear. Many designed sounds target these bands.

Be mindful of how you use this frequency range, though. It can be tempting to boost the mid and high frequencies to make sounds "pop," but while this may sound great on first listening, it may not age well if heard regularly, as many of our designed sounds are. Instead of making mid and high frequencies louder, look for opportunities to make the range clearer, more detailed, and free of distortion. Doing so increases the probability that the sound will be heard above background noise and makes it less likely to cause fatigue or distress.

PLAY WITH HARMONIC AND INHARMONIC SOUND COMBINATIONS

Harmonic overtones sound nice and pleasant, while *inharmonic* overtones provide complexity and contrast. The crash of cymbals is a prime example of inharmonic complexity. Bells and chimes often mix harmonic and inharmonic overtones in their sound: a percussive clang at the outset, followed by a more harmonic ringing with a gradual tapering off in volume.

If we say that a bell sounds "sparkly," it is because we are hearing harmonic overtones build up on top of a *fundamental frequency* (see Figure 3-8).

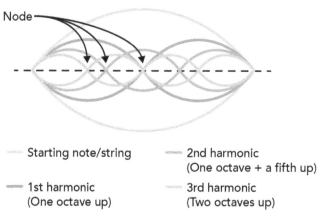

Node

| Starting note/string | 2nd harmonic
(One octave + a fifth up) |
| 1st harmonic
(One octave up) | 3rd harmonic
(Two octaves up) |

FIGURE 3-8
A string with a fundamental frequency (in yellow) and three overtones (in red, purple, and blue).

One way to understand the fundamental frequency and harmonic overtones is to imagine a jump rope. The fundamental frequency is the full length of the jump rope swung all the way around in a large arc for someone to skip. If you were to wiggle the jump rope in coordination with your partner on the other end, with some practice, you could produce "standing waves"—even divisions of the jump rope that "stand" in place as the rope spins around a node. Depending on how many nodes there are in the standing waves, you might have the first, second, or third harmonics. These harmonics sound nice when paired with the fundamental frequency because they're all even divisions of the fundamental.

Inharmonics, by contrast, have a certain "noisy" character (Figure 3-9).

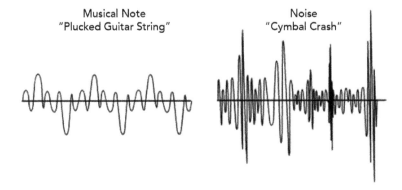

FIGURE 3-9

Inharmonics are noisy, nonrepeating waves. (Source: *http://zwmiller.com/projects/streamAudio.html*)

Inharmonic sounds function best as a kind of seasoning for sound. A little noisiness and harshness can be well employed, so long as it is not overused. Too many inharmonic frequencies will overpower a sonic experience, just as too much salt or pepper overpowers the taste of a dish—but just the right amount brings out the individual flavors in a beautiful and distinctive way.

WORK WITH VIBRATO

Vibrato refers to tiny variations in pitch within a sound. It is thanks to individual vibrato and tremolo (fine variations in loudness) that we can still identify individual voices within a choir, or perceive separate sources within synthesized sound. In his book *Music, Cognition and Computerized Sound* (MIT Press) Perry R. Cook writes, "There are styles of singing in which vibrato is suppressed as much as possible. Such singing has quite a different effect than typical Western European singing; when singers are successful in suppressing the vibrato to a sufficient extent, the chorus sound is replaced by a more instrumental timbre" or tone color. When we hear the simultaneous sound of many voices resonating without individualizing deviations, they literally become one: "The percept is not one of a group of singers but of a large complex instrument."[2]

WORK WITH TREMOLO

Amplitude is a measure of how much the air molecules move back and forth as a sound propagates through the air. It may also refer to how much the voltage must vary inside an electrical circuit to reproduce the sound electronically. For our purposes, we will use "amplitude" to refer to how quiet or loud a sound is.

How we manipulate loudness over time can drastically affect the way something sounds. A loud sound that drops off quickly, for example, will sound percussive, whereas if you want something that conveys the warmth of a human voice, small waverings in loudness—called *tremolo*—can help. The introductory section of the song "How Soon Is Now" by The Smiths offers an extreme version of synthesized tremolo.

CONSIDER HARMONIZING WITH THE CAVITY RESONANCE OF THE PRODUCT

Drum your knuckles on a hollow wooden box. The sound inside the box has a certain resonance. Different materials, sizes, and shapes all lead to particular frequencies of resonance. This adds to the character and quality of a product. When considering materials, remember that they impact how sound works both inside the product and outside. The shape of a container can work with or against the sounds coming from it. Anything with an enclosure made of plastic or thin metal that contains some empty space will exhibit cavity resonance. A mobile phone's cavity resonance adds to the sound it makes when it rings or buzzes.

Cavity resonance can be measured so that the sounds produced for the device can be tuned harmoniously to this frequency.

---

2 *Computerized Sound*, p. 34.

A Quick Method for Measuring Cavity Resonance

While this method is not a substitute for proper testing with the right tools, it will help you if you need to get a better idea of how the physical structure of a product will affect its auditory properties:

1. Set up a microphone.

   Set up a recording device next to the product. You're going to use this to record and then observe the output to diagnose the resonance of the product. Once you've recorded the files, you'll load the recording into a piece of software that allows you to look at its frequency.

2. Strike the product in multiple places and record the output.

   You can use any materials as long as they make a hard sound. Your knuckles or a rubber-tipped mallet are both good options.

   Strike the product in multiple spots so you can see how the experience of the product changes with the sounds played through it, and how the sound itself changes when played through the product. Look for the frequency of the largest peak after the initial transient (knuckle hit) from whacking it. If the parts are loose, they will vibrate against each other when the resonance is excited. Averaging these recordings results in a more accurate picture of the product's resonance.

   Create or find a *.wav* file of a sine wave that sweeps from 20 Hz to 20 kHz and back. Play this on the device.

   Record and review the two outputs for clues about resonant frequencies that emerge from the device.

   At certain frequencies, the device will rattle or produces "peaky" resonances. These give you a feel for the cavity resonance.

   Once you have clues to what the cavity resonance is, you can ensure that any tones that go into the product's audio will harmonize with this resonant frequency. The output is more likely to sound pleasing, because the cavity resonance can act as a harmonic overtone layered on top of the playout tones.

DESIGN WITHIN THE LIMITATIONS OF THE HARDWARE

It turns out that the brain can sometimes fill in missing harmonic information. You can create a chord by simply adding the third and fifth harmonics, and your brain will do the calculation and fill in the missing first fundamental.

This is an excellent trick that allows you to get amazing sound out of low-end hardware. When you listen to the effect on poorly made speakers, you can still *feel* and actually hear the sound of the lower harmonic, even though it's not there, because your brain adds it to your experience of the sound.

Listen to any of Paul McCartney's work with The Beatles from *Rubber Soul* onward for examples of this technique. Not only did it allow the "Beatles bass" sound to come through cheap speakers, it also gave the music part of its unique shape. Rather than hitting the root *dum dum dum dum* in a predictable fashion, McCartney *painted the space around the root*, giving it a profile and presence without having to actually play it.

You can also give sounds on cheaper hardware a little extra "oompf" by layering a low-frequency sine wave beneath the body of the sound. This is a popular technique in electronic music.

If you are working with particularly flimsy speaker hardware that not only lacks the ability to reproduce bass frequencies, but also weakly renders mid- and high-range frequencies, then try dirtying things up. Specifically, you can add small amounts of distortion and overdrive to create additional harmonics and fill out the sound.

DON'T GET STUCK ON "HIGH FIDELITY"

You approach an old Wurlitzer jukebox and drop in a coin. There are some clacking sounds from behind the glass as the record is pulled from a rack and placed on the turntable. The needle drops and you hear the characteristic needle sound—*ptsch thhhhhhhh*—coming from the speaker. The song starts with an electric guitar followed by vocals, drums, bass, and an electric organ.

The song was recorded in 1964, which means its entire signal path was analog. Among other things, this means no sampling rate, compression, information loss, or other issues associated with digital music. The sound exists as an analog waveform from production to playout.

The jukebox's stylus follows the grooves of the record and converts the physical pattern on the record to mechanical energy as it moves up and down. The movement is then converted to an electrical signal and then back into the movement of the speaker cone, and then the compression of the air.

If the stylus has not been changed in many years, it becomes dull, resulting in more distortion and high-frequency loss in audio playback. But the jukebox speaker makes a big sound. The cavity resonance of the jukebox's wooden cabinet emphasizes the bass, and the amplifier design results in a midrange boost. Although the high-frequency response would be described by most experts as "abysmal" and the harmonic distortion might cause eyes to water, none of this matters because by the time you hear the lyrics, you don't really care if this version of "House of the Rising Sun" is "low fidelity." Little imperfections go a long way toward making up the complex, emotional experience of listening to a song on a jukebox. In some cases, this beats a pair of perfect high-fidelity speakers. The rule is: if it sounds good, it is good.

COORDINATE HAPTIC, AUDITORY, AND VISUAL COMPONENTS

Haptics are created by tiny motors vibrating inside a product. You can think of them as sounds that are felt more than heard. They are great to employ when the auditory sense is blocked. You might not be able to hear something in a loud environment, but you can still feel it. Haptics can also bring life to auditory sounds. And they are more discreet than sounds, adding privacy to some interactions.

It is useful to coordinate the haptic, visual, and auditory elements of a device in a sophisticated manner. The Jambox portable speaker uses a haptic burst along with its signature startup sound, making the device feel more alive and less digital. Haptics can add rhythm and dimension to audio signals.

Paying attention to the way audio, visual, and haptics synchronize is a crucial part of getting the audio user experience right. A product with well-tuned sensory outputs is more likely to have a coherent identity. This is discussed further in Chapter 10.

OFFER MULTIPLE SOUNDSCAPES

When possible, give users a sonic palette and let them change the set of sounds associated with the product. It is likely we will see more options in soundscapes in the future. Similar to changing the theme on a website, this allows users to adapt the sounds to their own personal preferences. If you plan on doing this, aim for providing at least three choices. Giving users options can help a product stand out. Instead of locking someone into a specific interaction model, it offers some flexibility in experience. Personalizing the product to the user's own taste can bring greater satisfaction to the experience.

CONSIDER GENERATIVE AUDIO AND SONIFICATION

Generative audio and sonification, introduced in Chapter 1, are exceptionally useful for expanding the versatility of our audio alerts. Generative audio describes sound that uses programmed rules or live input to generate ever-changing sounds in real time. Sonification allows data and information to be encoded meaningfully into sound.

Generative audio can produce "endless" music, alerts, and sound effects that are nonrepetitive and unique. The advantage of generative audio is that it can create soundscapes or sequences of sound that the human brain doesn't get used to. Sonification and generative audio can be helpful in hospitals, where medical staff can overlook repetitive or uninformative alert sounds (we will discuss this in detail in Chapter 4). Tone color is an excellent way to leverage the power of generative audio. Instead of a sonic trademark playing back exactly the same way, a set of rules can make the sound play back a slightly different way each time.

Imagine:

- An alarm clock that begins your day with a familiar but ever-new, evolving alarm

- Devices that use machine listening to determine environmental sound levels to reduce or boost volume according to context

- An interface that models the physical properties of a container filled with liquid—instead of looking at a display, you rap on it with your knuckles and the resulting sound tells you if it is empty (*dommmmmp dommmmmp*) or full (*din din*); this could be used for battery life or anything else involving a quantity that varies

- Embedding information about the nature of a cardiac event using sonification

A simple application of generative audio and sonification can aid in all types of alert fatigue. Generative audio is often found in video game soundtracks, where the soundscape would otherwise be repetitive, but is still underutilized in sound for products. Instead of playing the same audio file each time the notification sounds, you can add a formula that adds varied sonic elements to the tone, or encode real information through sonification, so that the notification sounds unique every time you hear it. Instead of getting used to the alarm and ignoring it, your brain will hook onto the different elements and send the signal to respond.

Conclusion

When we design sound, we're more likely to make products that work for the long term rather than the short term, that add to people's lives instead of taking from them, and that are *embraced* instead of tolerated. Whether you are a designer, developer, device manufacturer, professor, student, entrepreneur, employee, or manager, you have an opportunity to fight for a good auditory experience for your product. If you do, you will find a better bottom line and more love from your customers!

There are many elements that can be used to make a sound stand out. We've talked about how to choose audio notifications for their intended context, and how to increase the variety, depth, and emotional reaction to sound through vibrato, frequency, tremolo, and overtones. This chapter also covers several larger ideas, such as audio that changes in real time to create variability, and sonification, which can be used to add more information to sound, allowing for more substance than a binary, on/off. Finally, we've included ways to consider how your sound interacts with the real world, through walls or other materials. With these tools, you will be able to create lasting, distinctive sounds.

[4]

Removing Sound from Interactions

THERE ARE MANY SITUATIONS where a sound doesn't match a context, volume, or environment. It is not always necessary to remove such a sound; sometimes it's sufficient simply to organize it. For example, we can organize sounds in a network of interconnected devices, such as those in a workspace, to keep them from interrupting at odd times.[1]

Removing or changing sounds into different senses can dramatically improve the user experience. This chapter provides a list of recommendations for removing sounds from interactions.

Unwanted Sounds

If you get annoyed when you hear the sound of someone chewing, you might have *misophonia*, or selective sound sensitivity syndrome. To people with this syndrome, specific sounds may incite feelings of stress, misery, or anger. Most of us have some sort of sound sensitivity. We might agree that many of the following sounds are *unwanted sounds*. They are annoying in some way, and we'd rather not hear them:

- Heavy in transients (snoring, noisy chewing and lip smacking, hacking coughs)

- Low frequency (sonic pressure of a large truck driving by)

- High frequency (squeaky wheels, chalk screeching on a chalkboard, children crying)

- Unexpected noise pollution (jackhammers, helicopters, steamrollers)

- Repetitive sound (service workers might hear the same 20 songs played over a sound system every day)

---

1 For more on mitigating interruptive technology, see Aaron Day, "Nash and the Noise: Using Iota to Mitigate Interruptive and Invasive Technology," *http://bit.ly/2RjNvP4*.

Employees that are exposed to higher levels of ambient sound are more likely to be sick, tired, stressed, and inefficient at communicating. Some standards organizations impose noise exposure limits for workplaces, but these standards are seldom sufficient in service, healthcare, childcare, or elder care industries, and are more often geared toward preventing acute health risks than creating a pleasant environment.

Let's look at a couple of examples of environments where sound could be reduced or removed to improve the lives of those experiencing it.

SOLVING ALARM FATIGUE IN HOSPITALS

[NOTE]

This section originally published by Kellyn Standley and Amber Case on Medium.com, "False Alarms and Alert Fatigue: The Tragic Design of Hospital Alerts," October 31, 2018.

Of the health hazards produced by technology in healthcare, alarm fatigue—or stress and desensitization from frequent alarms—frequently tops published lists.[2] Alarms keep patients awake at night, and some crucial ones are ignored when they sound too often. An astonishing percentage of alarms in hospitals are either false or clinically insignificant. These misleading alarms may be created by a mismatch between the default threshold for the alarm and the needs of the patient based on their size, age, and condition, or introduced through poor connectivity between sensors and the patient. The Joint Commission for Patient Safety reports: "The number of alarm signals per patient per day can reach several hundred depending on the unit within the hospital, translating to thousands of alarm[s] on every unit and tens of thousands of alarm[s] throughout the hospital every day."[3] Clinically insig-

---

2 Alarm fatigue has shown up on ECRI's yearly list of, "Top 10 Health Technology Hazards," every year since first being included in 2014, *http://bit.ly/2Omrg8Y*.

3 Joint Commission on Patient Safety, "Medical Device Alarm Safety in Hospitals," *https://www.jointcommission.org/assets/1/6/SEA_50_alarms_4_26_16.pdf*.

nificant alarms make up over 90% of pediatric ICU alarms and over 70% of adult ICU alarms.[4] An estimated 80-99% of ECG heart monitor alerts do not require clinical intervention.[5]

Hospitals are already noisy, chaotic environments, and the introduction of nuisance alerts can easily overwhelm workers (see Figure 4-1). If the equipment were calibrated and redesigned to reduce the number of clinically insignificant alarms, it would also reduce fatigue in workers.

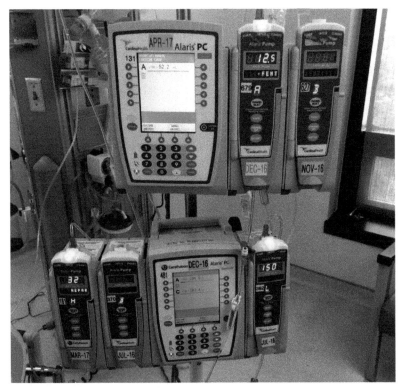

FIGURE 4-1

Some of the dozen machines with alarms and constant tones Amber Case's father was hooked up to in May 2016.

4 Amogh Karnik and Christopher P. Bonafide, "A framework for reducing alarm fatigue on pediatric inpatient units," PMC, *http://bit.ly/2SGiqWX*.

5 Samantha Jacques, PhD, and Eric Williams, MD, MS, MMM, "Reducing the Safety Hazards of Monitor Alert and Alarm Fatigue," PSNet, *http://bit.ly/2CXd0Bu*.

Medical devices are regulated by standards organizations that set requirements specifying that medical alerts must fit into specific frequency bands that target the most sensitive part of our hearing range. However, it is reasonable to believe this is simply an unfit approach for the context. Many of these devices meet legal requirements but still fail massively in experience design. The frequency and decibel requirements were set with the intention of enabling these alarms to be heard above background noise, however, when placed in a context of hundreds of such alarms, all sounding frequently, the intended purpose is overwhelmed by the number of alarms vying for attention.

While reducing the quantity of clinically insignificant alarms is a natural first step to mitigating the problem, rethinking the overall approach to sound design for these devices is essential. We explore some different strategies here. Some of these would require changes to the current regulations governing medical alerts, but others would not. Ultimately, converting to an integrated system and changing regulations seems well worthwhile, although it will take time to create a system that is sufficiently robust and well designed.

Because of the frequency with which healthcare workers are subjected to auditory notifications, they must be designed to be calm, positive, and relatively nonintrusive in order to not exhaust the faculties needed to answer them. To tie this back to principles mentioned in Chapter 3, the more often an alert or notification occurs, the less intense it should be. Also, for alerts that happen at irregular intervals, the notification should be longer. Because of their importance, it is likely that hospital alerts ought to be gentle but continuous until the underlying situation is addressed.

Could you imagine a joyful sound playing to bring a nurse or physician to a patient's room, instead of a harsh alarm? A beautiful and complex aria? Unless we block our ears or have limitations in our hearing, we cannot avoid hearing sounds. A melody would be difficult to miss, and we enjoy listening to beautiful things, so our inherent preferences should reinforce attention to such alarms rather than detracting. The new IEC 60601-1-8 guidelines for hospital alarms do allow for melodies,[6] but overt melody-making could run an additional risk of extreme annoyance from overuse. It may be better to borrow principles of ambient awareness and sonification to create a series of nonrepeating soundscapes that both calm and inform, disappearing seamlessly into the background but also creating a readable and digestible auditory text for practitioners.

One study of US hospitals showed that nurses take up to 40 minutes to respond to alarms,[7] and another showed caregivers responding to only 10% of alarms.[8] A further study demonstrated that, of all relevant alarms, caregivers could correctly identify only half of them.[9] A quieter hospital would help with patient recovery. Recognizable sounds, such as music or common sounds in nature, could help with identification. And overall, a positive connotation for any sound played in this context could reduce the emotional fatigue for both employees and patients. Design for alarms in healthcare must take the human element into consideration.

To reduce the cognitive load for doctors and nurses, more information could be placed into ambient awareness. With conscientious design, this could be formed into a "soundscape of health." We are arriving at a time where new capabilities in integrated devices are available to us. Instead of each manufacturer separately adding sound to just one device, we could instead integrate robust connectivity in each device (with a backup) in order to integrate sounds in a network.[10] This would allow the entire system to be sound-designed as a single cohesive auditory experience. This could be tailored to a particular specialty, culture, or location.

6 Dan O'Brien, "Audible Alarms in Medical Equipment," Medical Device and Diagnostic Industry, *https://www.mddionline.com/audible-alarms-medical-equipment.*

7 Sanderson PM, Wee A, Lacherez P., "Learnability and discriminability of melodic medical equipment alarms," NCBI, *https://www.ncbi.nlm.nih.gov/pubmed/16430567.*

8 Marie-Christine Chambrin, "Alarms in the intensive care unit: how can the number of false alarms be reduced?" NCBI, *https://www.ncbi.nlm.nih.gov/pmc/articles/PMC137277/.*

9 Cropp AJ, Woods LA, Raney D, Bredle DL, "Name that tone. The proliferation of alarms in the intensive care unit," NCBI, *https://www.ncbi.nlm.nih.gov/pubmed/8162752.*

10 For more discussion of this concept, see Aaron Day's "Nash and the Noise: Using Iota to Mitigate Interruptive and Invasive Technology," *http://bit.ly/2RjNvP4.*

It is likely that we will not be able to achieve a functional integration of hospital alarms without such an approach, which could be tackled with the type of dedication currently being applied to developing automated vehicles, although likely with fewer novel problems to solve, and therefore with fewer unknown technological hurdles. An interconnected system would enable greater context awareness for the machines. Context awareness is often critical to determining whether a particular reading is—or is not—clinically significant: "A heart rate of 170 on a treadmill test may warrant a low-priority condition whereas this same heart rate at an intensive-care monitoring station may be assigned a high priority."[11]

Additionally, an integrated system can analyze separate pieces of biometric data to generate condition-specific alarms, highlighting life-threatening conditions. For example, the Cushing response is a hardwired response to increased intracranial pressure, caused by a traumatic brain injury. It is a sign that there is a high probability of death within minutes or seconds. Cushing's response is indicated by decreased, irregular breathing, caused by impingement on brainstem function; low heart rate, caused by dysregulation of heart function; elevated blood pressure coupled with a widening of the difference between systolic ("on beat") and diastolic ("off beat") arterial pressures; and may be indicated by pathological waveforms, known as Mayer waves, on cardiac monitors. It occurs only in response to acute and prolonged elevations of intracranial pressure and the combination of elevated blood pressure and low heart rate occurred 93% *of the time* that blood flow to the brain dropped below key due to increased intracranial pressure.[12] It is a reliable indicator that requires immediate, life-saving intervention.

At present, Cushing's response is identified by healthcare workers actively attending to several independent alarms and visual displays and summing this information. Such a calculation on the part of the healthcare workers should be unnecessary. This response is both well understood and critical for care. It could easily be programmed into a

---

11 O'Brien, *https://www.mddionline.com/audible-alarms-medical-equipment.*

12 W.H. Wan, B.T. Ang, and E. Wang, "The Cushing Response: A Case for a Review of Its Role as a Physiological Reflex," *Journal of Clinical Neuroscience* 15 , no. 3 (2008): 223–228. doi:10.1016/j.jocn.2007.05.025. PMID 18182296

system of integrated devices, and such a system could take advantage of new scientific research and findings to further refine the diagnostic system and evolve a truly effective alert system.

An integrated system could also allow for automatic tailoring of the relevant thresholds for a particular patient using information entered into the hospital system, eliminating the time needed to individually customize alarm settings for each and every patient, as well as a large proportion of unnecessary alarms. An intelligent system could employ previous saved data to create an individual baseline, particularly when the patient has a special condition that presents with chronic irregularities that do not require clinical intervention. Devices could rely on listening and learning to coordinate their actions around the user, rather than the other way around.

Designing an evolving information soundscape could reduce alarm fatigue created by listening to the same type of constant, high-pitched beeps. Current guidelines for priority would be incorporated into the system, with a high priority given to alerts where death or irreversible injury could happen quickly, but a low priority if only discomfort or slow-developing conditions are likely. Soft background noises like crickets could indicate "all is well" in order to act as a steady-state indicator of a patient's biometric status, where the absence of such sounds indicates the need for an intervention, perhaps as a low-priority alert. Soft rhythms could indicate the pace of breathing or the current heart rate. This type of sonification could inform and unburden both caregivers and patients, allowing them to focus on important details. The advantage of direct sonification of data such as heart rate and breathing is that it directly translates the information and retains a high degree of specificity and variance. Over time, doctors and nurses will develop their ability to listen and be able to interpret elements that are not well conveyed by conventional alarms (emotional activation relates to heart rate and breathing, even though variations are understated). The soundscape would represent a true "fingerprint" for the patient, conveying multiple independent variables in a continuously generated composition.

A key insight from "Sonification" in Chapter 1 is that alerts need not carry a negative connotation in order to carry information. If additional meaning, such as priority level, can be added to an alert through nonstressful, emotionally neutral elements, such as increasing the tempo or the number of instruments in a composition (as with Brian Foo's sonification of income along the New York subway line in Chapter 1), then the alert becomes a special message decodable by doctors and nurses while remaining nonalarming and neutral to patients.

Another advantage of an intelligently integrated system is that it can employ localized sound through audio beamforming (also discussed in Chapter 1). This requires a system of smart speakers distributed around a room. It enables sounds to be set to different volumes in different parts of a room. This lessens the impact of alarm sounds on patients while still allowing them to be audible. Some sounds might be audible only when standing in a particular location, allowing the patient to rest in silence. Certain noncritical information, like the resting, ambient information about a patient, could be beamed right outside the room. Imagine doctors and nurses being able to listen outside of a patient's room to assess the patient's breathing rate, heart rate, blood glucose, and oxygen saturation. It could be a noninterruptive, calm way to assess a patient without even opening the door.

Integrating haptic signals sent to devices worn by doctors and nurses to signal critical, time-sensitive matters can ensure that important alarms are not missed. Haptics can be useful for anyone who may need to receive information without the use of their eyes and ears. They are a sensible backup to auditory notifications. Additional information could be conveyed in a coordinated fashion on a visual display, for instance, using devices like an Apple Watch or tablet. (See Chapter 8 for a more detailed discussion of switching notifications between hearing, sight, and touch.)

Even without changes to regulations, which an integrated system would require, much can be done to improve the quality and impact of hospital alerts. Redevelopment of medical equipment should focus on reducing connectivity issues between sensors and the patient, potentially by developing remote methods of monitoring the patient where they can be successful. Remote monitoring by measuring CO^2 released in breath is one promising avenue.[13]

---

13 B.D. Guthrie, M.D. Adler, and E.C. Powell, "End-Tidal Carbon Dioxide Measurements in Children with Acute Asthma," *Academic Emergency Medicine* 14, no. 12 (2008): 1135–9.

In many cases, sensors can be improved by simple user design, such as making them wireless, more discreet, and more comfortable to wear. Many sensors rely on a medical adhesive to maintain connectivity. If removing these sensors is uncomfortable for the patient, it is more likely the sensors will go unchanged for long periods of time, meaning the adhesive may dry out, which produces artifacts in the signals. A new adhesive could be an important breakthrough in increasing reliability of alarm signals and ease of use.

Another important change is simply to improve the playout hardware. As researchers have noted, "many pieces of medical equipment currently use low-cost piezoelectric audible alarms for their signaling. These are the same kind of alarms used in smoke detectors or at checkout counters at grocery stores. These low-cost alarms can no longer be used because they will not meet the complex frequency requirements of IEC 60601-1-8"—the new optional guidelines for medical equipment manufacturers as of 2006.[14] Low-quality speakers contribute to the cognitive burden on patients and healthcare workers by creating grating sounds.

A key element is allowing the sounds to be nonrepeating. A curious observation about human neurology is that our brains ignore sensations we receive too often. If we are constantly around a certain smell, such as a particular perfume, our brains will adapt to make it less apparent to us, to the point where it might altogether disappear from our conscious attention. If we get used to the sensation of glasses resting on our noses, we may forget we are wearing them, and if we hear the same sounds over and over our brains will start to filter them out. Generative audio, discussed in Chapter 1, would prevent habituation to specific sounds. The introduction of variability would make notifications more interesting, causing us to pay more attention. And because our minds naturally prioritize novel stimuli, even if the alerts are more subtle than beeping alarms, the lack of repetition should allow our brains to notice the sounds generated with more acuity and sensitivity.

The myriad of sounds we hear in nature is a good example of sounds that are clearly recognizable, yet change with each iteration. Using recognizable sounds from nature instead of abstract tones is one way

---

14 O'Brien, *https://www.mddionline.com/audible-alarms-medical-equipment.*.

we could aid memory and recognizability in alarms. Alternatively, because we are good at picking instruments such as trumpets, strings, and piano even out of a complex composition, it is not unreasonable to think that we could encode information in a constantly changing generative audio alert simply by creating rules about what trumpets signify, or string instruments, or piano.

Beyond coding alarms with information based on the instruments present in the composition, we could assign melodies to page individual doctors and nurses, which they could learn and over time would recognize instantaneously. In a hospital with such a system, instead of patients trying to block out interruptions from buzzing pagers and announcements, they would instead enjoy periodic melodies.

Companion technology to this system would of course be needed while the musical phrases and haptics were being learned. When the musical phrases became known, doctors and nurses would have difficulty not noticing when they were played. This companion system would provide an alternative for people with hearing impairments and a backup if the system goes offline. A pager, phone, or smartwatch could display the meaning of the messages in text and buzz to alert users.

The cacophony of beeps we have created as hospital alarms is simply poor design. It is ineffective and counterproductive. Let us imagine a better, more healthful hospital system.

AMBIENT SOUND IN ANIMAL ENVIRONMENTS AND HABITATS

Although we talk about sound exposure in work environments for humans, sound design for animals is often overlooked. It is essential to empathize with the creatures that live alongside us. Animals can't change their environments like we can. The noise from dog kennels can reach above 100 decibels. Fish and amphibians can be disrupted by the noisy pumps and motors in their tanks. This results in shortened lifespans and miserable quality of life.

Simple acoustic treatment for these spaces can dramatically improve the experience of animals and those that work with them. Quieting pumps and tank components or accessories can improve conditions for these sensitive creatures. We can work to understand their particular needs and help them live full and enriched lives.

In some cases, adding sounds to animal environments can be help-ful for desensitizing animals to sounds associated with human com-pany. Particularly for animals like rabbits and guinea pigs, but also for feral cats and abused animals, sounds from children's movies can help familiarize animals with background noise including language and music, which can make them calmer when in the presence of people.

Guidelines for Removing Sound from Interactions

In this section we'll look at specific guidelines for removing sound from common user interactions with your products.

ENABLE USERS TO TURN OFF THE SOUND OR CHANGE THE NOTIFICATION STYLE

Consider how a sound might disrupt others or go off when unnecessary. Some insulin pumps have beeps that cannot be turned off or reduced in volume. These lifesaving devices might not be heard in loud environ-ments, and might disrupt others in quiet ones. Allowing users to switch the notifications to a vibration can help prevent contextual mismatch.

ELIMINATE REDUNDANT NOTIFICATIONS WHEN POSSIBLE

Consider removing or "downgrading" sounds where they might be unnecessary or redundant. This will lighten the cognitive load on the user and unify the sensory aspects of the product experience. Consider the sound's default volume, whether the sound builds over time (like a teakettle), and whether or not the sound can be turned off by the user.

PAIR SOUNDS WITH HAPTICS

Consider how to pair sound with haptic stimuli, including timing and rhythm. Language and voice can often be converted to tones, and tones can often be converted to lights or haptics. Be creative.

ENSURE SOUNDS FIT WITHIN THE CONTEXT

You cannot fully anticipate the context in which your product will be used. The more intrusive a sound is, the more control the user should have over the *way* it will intrude.

Imagine setting a dishwasher late at night and having a noisy alert dis-turb your sleep. Some home appliances, like washers and dryers, allow users to turn off the sounds entirely. Here is a set of considerations for making sounds flexible:

- Allow the user to change the volume of the sound via an easily accessible volume setting.

- Give the user the ability to turn the sound off—ideally, for each notification individually and with a single control that mutes everything. However, if a sound is associated with critical machinery (such as construction equipment, or back-up sounds for electric vehicles), it is important that it is built to be unalterable.

- Add a setting where users can set a time range during which the product won't make a sound. For example, Apple's iPhone has a Do Not Disturb mode that ceases notifications at a specific time of day. It is important to allow the range to be set—don't assume everyone has the same sleep schedule. Late-night or swing-shift workers might have different noise reduction needs.

- Allow users to change the sound into a different type of notification, such as a haptic (touch/vibration) or light signal. Converting to a haptic notification is often a perfect solution for personal devices that are naturally close to the body, since haptic signals are mainly perceptible by the intended recipient, not those around them. This kind of change can help give users control over wearable medical devices such as insulin pumps (which often come with sounds that cannot be switched off), and is especially useful if the notification is critical to life support. Relying solely on sound can be dangerous when the user is in a loud environment and unable to hear the alert, and can cause problems during movies or funerals, for example.

CHECK THAT THE FREQUENCY MATCHES THE CONTEXT

Humans naturally localize high-frequency, short-duration sounds such as clicks, and the human ear is most sensitive to sounds in the 2–4 kHz range. These sounds can be used for urgent, unmissable alerts that occur relatively infrequently (such as fire alarms), but if your product doesn't require this kind of notification, consider using a different range of frequencies or ambient soundscapes and background notifications. In certain cases, such as construction and medical alerts, ISO guidelines constrain alerts to specific frequency ranges. Check the parameters of your project before designing out of the box.

REDUCE NOISE FROM MECHANICAL SOURCES

Operating noise is one of those qualities that can make or break that hard-to-define "feel" of a product. If you're designing consumer electronics, appliances, or other products that contain motors or transformers, or require cooling, put some thought into the unintended sources of sound. It's often worth the small additional expense to use a quieter fan, for example, or to include sound-dampening measures to reduce a product's unintended sonic footprint.

CONSIDER ACTIVE NOISE CANCELLATION TECHNOLOGY

Many modern headphones use *active noise cancellation* to reduce the effects of noise. Versions of this technology are used in telepresence systems as well as mobile devices and laptops. Active noise cancellation comes at a cost of some distortion to the signal it is protecting against noise, but it does reduce the overall fatigue users can experience from the constant pressure of high decibels, and it can make certain products and experiences much more tolerable.

REDUCE THE VOLUME OF THE ALERT

The simplest fix for intrusive sounds may be simply to decrease their volume. For example, the sound when a user presses a start button on an electric kettle need not be as loud as the sound announcing that the water is ready. It may not be the nicest-sounding beep, but we have, with this simple change, gone from "bad" to "not bad."

This is a simple example of what we mean by paying attention to context. Even though both sounds are made by the same device and heard by the same person, they occur in different contexts, which can be predicted with a bit of thought and attention. A "set" alarm always occurs when the user is next to the device, while a "boil" alarm usually happens when the user is at a distance. Taking this simple fact into account allows for a much more satisfying, humane audio user interface.

A kettle in an industrial kitchen shouldn't need sounds at all; it is already a complex environment. The kettle could instead have a visual indicator and the option to turn on a sound if needed. Ideally, in a home the sound can be made louder if the house is large. If it's a tiny condo, you should able to turn the sound down or off.

REMOVE OR REDUCE SPEECH

Speech is more cognitively expensive to process than a simple tone. An in-car navigation system is a more reasonable use of speech than a robotic vacuum cleaner. Consider whether spoken words are absolutely necessary to your product. Replace speech with tones, lights, or short melodies, and consider replacing tones with haptic alerts or small indicator lights. Downgrade speech to alerts, or alerts to lights, to reduce cognitive burdens on your users.

Conclusion

Products don't always need reductions in sound, but when they do, consider changing the alert style or volume, and providing the ability to turn the sound off. Test your product in a variety of contexts, including late at night, when the cost of intrusion could be higher than during the day. Finally, consider what happens when things go wrong, and how your product might work smoothly alongside people—or animals—in everyday life. You are never going to be able to predict all of the contexts in which your product might be used, but allowing users to change how it sounds is the best way of ensuring that they can adequately adapt it to their needs.

[5]

Sound and Brand

A SONIC TRADEMARK IS a relatively short piece of audio that does for your sound brand what a visual trademark does for your visual identity: it serves as a single, memorable reference point that gives customers something to grab onto when thinking about your product or brand. For dipping your foot into these audio logos, few places are better to start than by watching Wired's video, "The Psychology Behind the World's Most Recognizable Sounds."[1] Here, sound designers explain the effect of some of the most familiar digital sounds on us, including startup sounds, ringtones, and audio logos.

The *boink-spoosh* of Skype starting up is a good example. It is probably the first thing you think of when asked what Skype "sounds" like, but Skype also makes lots of other sounds that reflect a similarly playful mood. Further, part of Skype's "sound" comes from the technical methods it uses to compress human voice.

But note that a sound trademark is a subset of the auditory brand experience, not its entirety. Take the Macintosh, for example: the rich, warm chord it plays upon startup might be the most memorable part of its sound experience, but there is also the fan sound, the sound of the mouse and keyboard, and the sound quality that is shaped by the particular speakers hardwired into the machine. All of these elements come together to create a unique soundscape that aligns with the visual and interactive components of the brand.

Whether or not you attempt to design the sound in your product to fit its brand, the sound will be there—even if your product contains no electronics whatsoever. Some brands have sounds that are based on the shape of their packaging or the product itself. The *snap, crackle,*

---

1 Watch the video: *https://www.youtube.com/watch?v=S_gBMJe9A6Q&t=5s.*

pop of Kellogg's Rice Krispies is so iconic that it has become part of the product's branding. In Germany, a crucial part of the brand identity of Flensburger Pilsener beer is the characteristic *plopp!* sound that its unique bottles make when opened. Even an ordinary wooden cabinet makes a sound when struck or moved, and this becomes a part of its identity.

Think of an old piece of furniture in your house: their sonic signatures are part of the memories you form about them. As we've covered in previous chapters, environments also present many (usually overlooked) opportunities for sound to be added, shaped, or removed, and this can support a brand identity over longer periods of time.

When we get to products that actively produce sound, like apps and smart devices, the potential sources proliferate dramatically. So, it's worth starting out by cataloging, in very broad terms, the sources of sound that ultimately influence a customer's experience of whatever you're designing.

For *physical and digital products*, this includes:

- *Passive elements*, such as product enclosures, which both shape the sounds within them and communicate many qualities about the product when touched, tapped, or knocked

- The *electronics* that make or modify sounds, such as voice chat applications

- *Mechanical and electromechanical components* such as cooling fans, doorbells, electronic locks, or anything with a motor, switch, or servo in it

For *environments*, this includes:

- The *electronics* that make or modify sounds, such as public address systems or background music

- *Mechanical and electromechanical systems*, such as heating and cooling systems, transformers, or keycard door locks

- *Passive elements*, such as wind chimes or floor surfaces (when walked upon), but especially architectural acoustics, which contribute tremendously to the identity of a space

Finally, does your product have an *essence?* Some things have a face, others a voice, and a lucky few have an essence: something that emerges when all the sensory information we gather about a product is coherent. When the experiential touchpoints—context, look, feel, sound, heft, scale, and so forth—fit together well, a product is more likely to have an identifiable individual character.

Every aspect of your brand should feel like it came from the same place, and this includes sound. Many audio branding efforts fail for the simple reason that too much emphasis is placed on the sound trademark or "logo," and not enough on creating a balanced multisensory brand experience.

As competitors release products into the marketplace, the task of creating a distinctive identity becomes more difficult. Sound is a crucially overlooked tool in this task.

Anything that produces sound is part of your brand. That includes keystrokes on a computer keyboard, the acoustics of tapping on the device itself, the internal components in the motor, and what it sounds like to drop it, eat it, open it, unwrap it, or use it.

If your aim is to use sound to improve the experience of using the product in a way that reinforces existing brand characteristics, then your strategy should start with sensitivity and empathy toward your customers' needs and expectations.

Intel Audio Logo

Austrian-born composer Walter Werzowa took a simple concept to develop the most well-known audio logo in the world: Intel. It was also one of the first. With a background of creating longer compositions, Werzowa was pulled in to help a friend complete a job. His friend had drafted the keyframes for a three-second animation of the Intel logo spiraling together, and said, "This is three seconds of music." There were no audio logos out there. Just tons of jingles about 30 seconds long about how tasty Coke was, or Oscar Meyer wiener or Kit Kat bar. Werzowa's first reaction was to crack up: "Driving home from the studio I was thinking, 'Three seconds—that is just impossible. Why would someone need that?'"

That weekend, Werzowa scoured through his musical scores from The Beatles, Mozart, and even Jimi Hendrix to see if there was any three-second musical phrase out there that just made sense. But nothing did. On Sunday he began to get really worried, and put the animation boards back up. "I was reading 'In-tel In-side' as the tagline. If this was a song, it would be four notes. This is for engineers, so it should be probably an even, rather than syncopated rhythm, like four eighth notes. Then if I think of global impact, the most powerful, open intervals are the fourth and the fifth."

Werzowa says he got lucky in talking about the concept first before he played it to the stakeholders. Especially at the time, there was no research about how powerful audio logos could be. Audio logos need to have a story that supports the company's ethos and brand. If you simply play the melodies, it is unlikely stakeholders will hear their brand name in the melody.

The complexity and memorability of the Intel logo came out of the evolution of that simple idea. They worked on the Intel sound for another couple months, making it more electronic or less electronic, and adjusting different aspects of the sound. Werzowa emphasizes how important it is for people to have something to grab onto. Give composers lots of freedom to develop what they feel it should be, but the dialogue with stakeholders is important—really talk about what your brand is.

Types of Trademarks

A sound trademark will contain at least one or more of the following features:

- Rhythmic structure: a "beat" or identifiable rhythmic pattern

- Unique tone color (timbre)

- A melody or motif; this is by far the most popular implementation

- A chord or series of chords producing harmony

- A spoken voice or series of words

RHYTHM-BASED TRADEMARKS

Example: Siemens

Bam-pa, bom! Taa-TAA troot! Ba-deedle-dee-paa-dooop! Some trademarks consist of a rhythmic structure, a "beat" or identifiable rhythmic pattern.

Advantages

If the rhythm is strong enough it can "carry" any kind of sound and still be recognizable. Put another way, rhythm *degrades* well. Even if the sounds that make up the rhythm are obscured or distorted, the rhythm will still be recognizable.

Rhythms are also *sticky*. For example, once you have heard the mnemonic "right-y tight-ee, left-y loose-y," it is hard to forget.

Disadvantages

It can be difficult to design a rhythm that's unique enough to be identifiable while also being discreet, especially in a short time frame. In other words, unless you play it loud or there are loud periodic components, it can get lost in environmental noise more easily than other trademarks.

TONE-COLOR BASED TRADEMARKS

Examples: Windows 95, Windows NT, Sony PlayStation, and Xbox startup sounds

Every sound is composed of spectra that contain harmonic and inharmonic sounds. Just like a fingerprint, each of these tone colors, or *timbres*, is unique.

It is the tone color that makes an oboe sound like an oboe, a violin sound like a violin, and a clarinet sound like a clarinet. It is what we are describing when we use words like *glassy*, *reedy*, or *woody*; it is the precise fingerprint of the harmonic and inharmonic overtones that an instrument produces with each note.

Advantages

It is easy to make a tone color–based trademark unique. There are a limited number of ways you can glue together a short melody, but an infinite number of possible colors of sound. Tone color audio logos would pair well with generative audio. Instead of playing back exactly the same, a set of rules could allow the sound to be played back in a recognizable, but subtly different way each time. This would be a unique approach to a sonic trademark.

Disadvantages

You cannot hum, sing, or whistle it (at least not without difficulty). It needs a minimum quality of playout hardware. A unique tone color might not be recognizable when played on low-quality speakers.

MELODY-BASED TRADEMARKS

Examples: T-Mobile/Deutsche Telekom, Intel, Nokia, NBC

Melody-based trademarks are the most memorable and most commonly thought of trademarks. Beyond familiarity, melody has a lot going for it. Melodies are extremely portable—they can be sung or whistled, for example—and this matters tremendously in the battle for attention.

Advantages

Melodies are also "tone–color–independent." For the most part, it does not matter what kind of sound you use, as long as it has a periodic wave-form, and more tonal content than noise. For example, whether it is a marching band or a melody-playing dot-matrix printer playing it, you can identify the T-Mobile/Deutsche Telekom *da da da DEE da*.

Disadvantages

It can get old fast. In musical terms, a great many logos use some version of the I, II, IV, and V intervals (this is worth looking up if you're curious—it's pervasive in Western music traditions) to try to sound either "perky-happy" or "majestic-comforting." But what makes something familiar can also make it irritating. If it sounds annoying, it *is* annoying.

CHORD- OR HARMONIC-PROGRESSION–BASED TRADEMARKS

Examples: Macintosh startup sound, THX audio logo

Advantages

Similar to melody, chord- and harmonic-based trademarks can function independently of specific tone colors.

Disadvantages

Also like melodies, repeated harmonies can become tiresome if over-used. Many harmonies or progressions default to some combination of I, II, IV, and V intervals. It might make sense from the perspective of psychoacoustics, as these are positive progressions, but in the long run, if it sounds cheesy, it is.

SPOKEN-WORD–BASED TRADEMARKS

Examples: General Mills's "Ho! Ho! Ho! Green Giant," Yahoo!

Advantages

There are relatively few spoken word trademarks out there, and if effective, they can increase the memorability of the name of your company, or your motto. Spoken-word trademarks, such as General Mills's "Ho! Ho! Ho! Green Giant" or Yahoo!'s "yah-HOOOOO," are just sounds of a particular shape, color, and duration.

Disadvantages

They can be cheesy or distracting. Because language takes more attention than sounds, spoken word audio logos may not be as calm or unintrusive.

MULTI-FACETED AUDIO TRADEMARKS

Many trademarks combine more than one element. The 20th Century Fox sound trademark, for example, starts with a recognizable marching snare (rhythm), followed by brass instruments and strings playing a chord progression.

The upward steel guitar *bwwoooing* of Looney Tunes cartoons is an excellent example, which is identifiable by its timbre but then switches to a melody. THX starts with a unique tone color and ends with a majestic chord. However, there will always be one feature that cannot be removed—this is what we might consider the *spine* of the trademark.

General Advice for Sound Trademarks

In this section, we'll present some general advice to keep in mind when designing sound trademarks.

MAKE IT FUTURE-PROOF

How long do you expect your product to be around? A well-built blender might last for 10–20 years, but software and digital hardware is often traded in every year or two.

To hit a moving target, you need to aim ahead of the current market. Will you be able to switch out sound for your product via a software update? If so, this isn't a huge risk and allows for more experimentation. But if your sound is "locked in" to the hardware, know that using sounds associated with a particular music style or design aesthetic might sound dated rather quickly. Think it through before committing the latest sonic memes to your product.

MAKE IT INTERESTING

Use tone color. A more harmonically complex sound is going to stand the test of time more successfully than a simple one.

MAKE IT SHORT

Brevity wins. As a general rule of thumb, the length and intensity of a sound should be inversely proportional to the frequency of its occurrence.

Most sonic logos have a duration of one to five seconds, although there are exceptions. If a piece of software takes a little while to load, a calm, meandering, long ambient sound could be associated with it. The length of this sound can provide a distraction during the loading time. Other examples are the 20th Century Fox and THX trademarks, which take advantage of their more or less captive movie audiences.

MAKE IT POLITE

Make your audio logo recognizable at any reasonable volume, but don't rely on forcing the user's attention.

CONSIDER THE SENSITIVITY OF HUMAN EARS

Humans are more sensitive to some frequencies than others. Match the sound to the context, and don't overwhelm the human ear with sounds in the same frequency range. Sounds in critical bands are often overused.

MAP OUT THE COMPETITIVE BRANDSCAPE

Do some homework and examine what others are doing so you can position your audio logo accordingly. You might need to place your mark in the same emotional space as your competitor in order to leverage the power of association, or you might prefer to strike out into uncharted lands to find a place where none have gone before. You can use the dichotomies listed in Table 5-1 to inform your direction.

TABLE 5-1. Dichotomous terms used to describe sound

Spacious	Closed
Resolution	Tension
Natural	Synthetic
Classic	Contemporary
Unique	Familiar
Simple	Complex
Woody	Plastic
Hollow	Dense
Consonance	Dissonance
Phrased (example: *womple-di-domple-dy*)	Exclaimed (*peng!*)
Thick	Thin
Longer	Shorter
Smooth	Sharp
Moving pitches	Static pitches
Literal	Abstract
One part	Many parts

One approach is to start with an attribute matrix or two (see Figures 5-1 through 5-4). This is a fast, easy way to get a feel for the sonic "brand-scape" and look for positioning opportunities. Furthermore, most companies' brand departments will understand this tool.

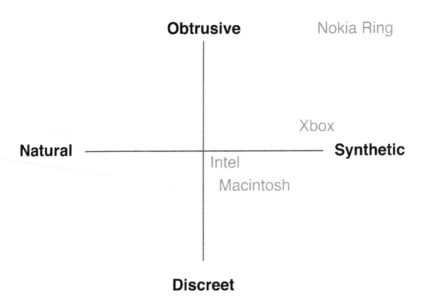

FIGURE 5-1
Classic brand sounds on an axis of obtrusive to discreet and natural to synthetic.

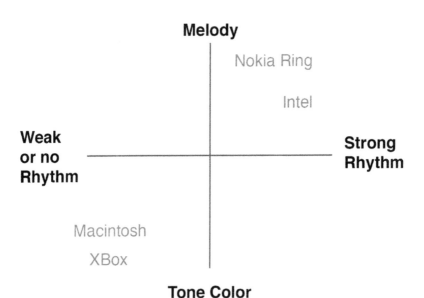

FIGURE 5-2
The same sounds on an axis that contrasts rhythm with melody and tone color.

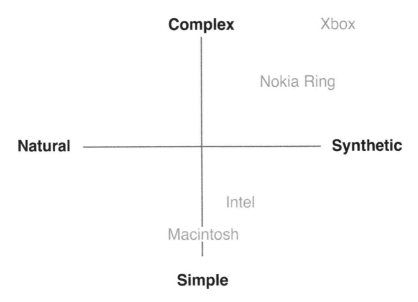

FIGURE 5-3
The same audio logos on a scale of natural to synthetic, simple to complex.

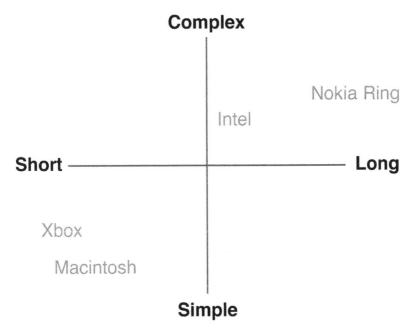

FIGURE 5-4
The same audio logos on a scale of complex to simple and short to long.

After laying out the attribute matrix and choosing the style of audio logo, you will use this information to create a design brief, described in Chapter 8, to complete the specification of what you want in your audio logo. Hopefully you will create an enduring and recognizable sonic identity for your brand.

Conclusion

Start with sensitivity and empathy toward your customers' needs and expectations, and you will be far more likely to be successful with your sound branding efforts.

The more senses you get right, the better the overall experience your customers will have! Never lose sight of the fact that your customers, and the people they know and love, may have to hear that sound repeatedly, for years or even decades. This can be a source of praise or of frustration.

If, after spending months on a sound branding project, you're able to declare that an upward swooshing sound symbolizes *innovation* and an F major chord from an expensive Steinway piano connotes *experience*— and it elicits a positive reaction from the customers who hear it—then your hard work was worth it.

Designing Voice Interfaces

VOICE INTERFACES ARE A huge and booming area of development. Consumers have more options than ever before, from Amazon Alexa and Google Home to Siri and Cortana. Voice interfaces are found in vehicles, appliances, and televisions, and in third-party partnerships with restaurant booking systems, maps, and home-speaker systems.

Vocal Persona

Designing a vocal persona is as important as designing the response model for the voice interface. Voice interfaces can borrow lessons on timing, personality, and character from theater, improv, and comedy. Studying improvisation can help with building conversation-based interactions, such as the "yes and" rule of improv theater. Start by describing the attributes you would like your vocal persona to convey, and work through exercises from different disciplines for inspiration.

Our expectations for voice interfaces have been heavily influenced by the television and film industry. TV shows and movies such as *Star Trek: The Next Generation*, *Star Wars*, and *Dr. Who* have depicted how we might communicate with devices, like robots, as individuals. For example, *Star Wars*'s C3PO android might be fluent in over 6 million forms of communication, but he is regarded as bothersome in every one, whereas R2D2's tone-based *BEEP BOOP* language conveys emotion, personality, and information without a spoken word, and he is regarded as adorable. Figure 6-1 maps out different verbal and nonverbal robot personas used in popular films and household products, and whether they are considered sinister or benevolent.

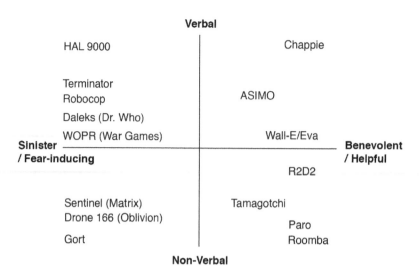

FIGURE 6-1
Verbal and nonverbal robot personas

All of these personalities rely on tone color and timing to indicate intent. Chappie's friendly but modulated South African accent (coupled with his expressive "ears" and eyebrow) identifies his character as the opposite of the sinister but monotone HAL, or the shrill and threatening Dalek.

What else differentiates Chappie from a Dalek? Although Chappie's voice was processed to sound "robotic," its pitch varied, and it was higher and youthful-sounding. The Dalek's voice was processed with a ring modulator and the Cylon's with a vocoder, creating a droning metallic sound.

Use timing

Timing is a major differentiator. Motion pictures rely heavily on suspense to engage the viewer. This is fine if we are at the cinema, but less so when we're interacting with products. So, unless you want a product with HAL's personality, you should avoid pregnant pauses.

There are quite a few examples in the sinister and verbal quadrant. Robots in this category are not necessarily aggressive. They may simply say something benign but ill-timed that unsettles viewers. One example is HAL's response to a desperate astronaut: "I'm sorry, Dave, I'm afraid I can't do that." On the other hand, a Dalek's terse scream of "Exterminate!" is overtly threatening, intrusive, and persistent.

On the other hand, Google Duplex add "ums" and other conversational fillers (known as *dysfluencies*) to make it seem more human and give the person on the other end time to respond. You may not want this kind of voice concatenation and speech in something like Alexa, where you want an immediate, precise response. During a conversation where people need to look up things and go back and forth in conversation, however, these disfluencies actually *improve* communication, by allowing the software to indicate it is still listening, thinking about a question, or taking time to process a complex sentence. It works on the other (human) end in the business context because it gives people time to look up things or consult schedules.

Work with intonation

Sounds with changing pitch can mimic speech patterns in some languages. Consider the following conversation between C3PO and R2D2 from *Star Wars: Episode IV—A New Hope*, in which C3PO is admonishing R2D2 in English, while R2D2 responds with his characteristic analog synthesis whistle and chirp:

> **R2D2:** Qua-wheeep? *[A "hopeful" sound whose pitch moves up, a common characteristic of asking questions in English.]*

> **C3PO:** No, I don't think he likes you at all.

> **R2D2:** Qua-whoooo? *[Pitch goes less than half of the previous sound—sounds a bit like "really?"]*

> **C3PO:** No, I don't like you either.

> **R2D2:** Wooooooo. *[Pitch goes down, like "Ohhhh."]*

It might be easy to assume, then, that pitch up means positive and pitch down means negative. In many cases this holds true, but only for part of the world. We haven't considered tonal languages like Mandarin. Although all verbal languages use pitch to express information, tonal languages can differentiate words—in particular monosyllabic words—simply by changing pitch and tone.

More advanced development may include multiperson identification, using biometrics to determine who is speaking from a set of known users, and arbitration between multiple devices. In this book, we will focus on the elements that impact the personality of the voice in voice user interfaces. For more information about how to develop the entire interface, refer to Cathy Pearl's book *Designing Voice User Interfaces: Principles of Conversational Experiences* (O'Reilly). This book can guide you through basic voice interface design principles, help you choose the right speech recognition engine, and help you understand, improve, and measure the performance of your interface.

Remember that it takes time to fine-tune sounds and voices so they have the intended effect. It comes down to details. Use a lot of prototypes along the way, and leave plenty of time to refine your work at the end of the project.

Conclusion

Sound gives products a voice, and every voice has an inherent personality. The best voice user interface feels like a natural extension of your social circle. Because we evolved communicating with other humans, speaking to a voice interface can feel more seamless than interfaces that require typing, pressing buttons, or turning a dial.

In addition, voice interfaces are language-specific, which carries a risk of miscommunication. If a voice alert is in a single language, such as an automated boarding call, a percentage of listeners might not understand it. In these cases, it is important to ensure there a back-up method of communication, such as a text message or visual display.

Part II

The Sound Design Process

[7]

Interviewing

THE INTERVIEW STAGE SHOULD give you a good feel for what's possible, and for the overall scope of the project. After this, you should be prepared for an audit of what's already been built, and of expectations for the product. Performing this quick review of the problem space is essential for discovering a project's constraints and time frame. From hardware, frequency range, and tone to schedule, scope, and user experience, each aspect of the project needs to be fully investigated.

Share knowledge, ask questions, and manage expectations. By identifying and clustering the problems that need to be solved through the removal or addition of sound, you'll find that the nature of the design space as a whole starts to take shape.

If the product is new or if you're working with a startup, not all of the interviewing process covered in this chapter will be applicable, but it should still be a useful guide to direct your work.

Interviewing Stakeholders

If you are creating interfaces for a product or service, you are obligated to find out what kinds of sounds it makes or will make. You will need to investigate and go deep. If you are not an engineer for the project, talk to someone who is and find out what they know. Take stock of the things you can influence, as well those you cannot, bearing in mind that other brands or corporate entities might be playing sounds through your device as well. In the end, sound for interfaces deserves at least as much scrutiny as its visual and interactive counterparts.

You'll want to do interviews within the organization to see what's needed. You'll also want to do preliminary user studies. Together, these will give you enough information to create a deliverables document to use as the basis for product development.

Communication between groups is essential. A good interview feels like a conversation, and can be a powerful tool for creating shared expectations. Solicit not just the facts, but the dream as well. Have people tell you what their vision would sound like if money were no object. You may discover new use cases or get new ideas from your counterparts. Even if interviewees are uncommunicative, this alerts you to possible friction in getting buy-in from them or their team.

Not everyone in the room will share a background in audio or have time to understand audio-specific terminology. If they don't have a vocabulary with which to describe sound, they might be cautious or defensive when discussing it. Communicate and define the terms that you'll use, and let them do the rest. Use the definitions at the beginning of this book to help expand participants' vocabulary.

Determining the Scope of Work

Design projects can vary widely in terms of scope. You will find that your deliverables will fit into one of the following categories:

A single design
> This is usually something like a sound trademark (see Chapter 5) or a single audio branding element such as a startup sound or alarm. This isn't necessarily limited to additive sound design. You might be asked to take an existing design and make it fit the experience better. In some cases you might discover that a subtractive approach is best, as described shortly.
>
> Working on a single design can be extremely rewarding. Not only do you get a chance to hone your skills, but these are also opportunities to try out new design ideas. Your experiments might not get selected for further development, but testing ideas within the initial client review can help you discover what processes are worth spending your time developing.

A comprehensive auditory experience for a product
> This is the complete auditory experience or sound design for a product. It includes all interactions with the device.

A comprehensive auditory experience for an environment

Comprehensive designs for exhibits, hospitals, and other environments are highly satisfying. They are an order of magnitude more complex than single designs or designs for projects. This isn't for technical reasons, but because you'll be working with a wide range of people with their own agendas and concerns.

A family of auditory experiences

This is when you are designing sound for a range of products—for example, all the different microwave ovens from a manufacturer, or all the human–machine interfaces (HMIs) for an automotive manufacturer. These projects need a core team of at least two people, with one devoted exclusively to communication.

There are many different versions of this problem. However, they have one thing in common you can't afford to ignore: you need to break up the problem into manageable pieces and commit to calling each of those pieces "done" as soon as you can. Instead of building something that you can't test until after you have spent a lot of time and budget, distribute your risk by working on short, achievable goals. Then if something goes haywire, the sunk costs are low.

Subtractive deliverables

A noisy electromechanical experience, such as a blender or vehicle, might come with requirements for specific decibel levels or an overall reduction in unwanted noise, and an annoying set of sounds may come with recommendations for simplification and reduction. For mechanical cases, you'll need to work with a larger team of engineers and materials scientists to determine how to cancel, remove, or improve existing sounds within the constraints of an existing or new product. For a user interface, subtracting audio components may be as simple as lowering the volume or trading audio for visual notifications or haptics.

Interview Questions

When you first meet with stakeholders, you'll need to get as much information as you can. Try to get answers to the more general questions before you write your proposal. Even if you receive a detailed request for proposal, it's helpful to ask some clarifying questions.

Interview internal partners, clients, and suppliers. This is also the stage where you will discover other people related to the project who are excited about the auditory experience of their product.

STAKEHOLDER QUESTIONS

- What decisions do you need run by you?
- How much information and detail would you ideally like to receive about the process?
- Who else needs to be involved?
- What are your aspirations for the project?
- What do you want it to "feel" like?
- What would you want to create if money were no object?
- How quickly does the product need to go to market?

TECHNOLOGY LIMITATIONS AND SPECIFICATIONS

- If the product is software-based, will it be expected to operate on a variety of platforms? What kind of playout hardware will be used on each platform?
- What sample rates and bit depths does it support? Remember that you'll want to design sounds that work well at different sample rates.

[TIP]

For more about working within hardware limitations, see Chapter 10.

- Does the product support stereo or mono playout? If the audio is mono, and you've mixed it for left and right channels, you might have phase cancellation when it plays back as mono. To avoid this, test with and design for the target hardware.

- What kind of physical interface does the product use? Is it a touch-screen? If so, is it capacitive or resistive? Capacitive touchscreens are more responsive than resistive touchscreens; resistive touch-screens may need to be tested for adequate response time during frequent interaction.

- Will the sounds be prerecorded, or will they be generated in real time?

- Does the product have the capability to use haptics and not just sounds?

- Does the product have a machine-listening component? If so, is there a privacy policy in place for data usage? Is there a hard "off" switch for the machine-listening component? What happens in the case of a hardware exploit?

MATERIALS

- What materials are being used in the product?

- How might these materials influence the sound of the product?

- What inspiration can the materials lend to the sound?

INTERACTION TIMES AND TRIGGERS

- What triggers the interaction? How long are interaction times?

- Is an audio element expected with every interaction? Can the user turn the audio element off, or is it a legal requirement of the design? (Devices in the healthcare industry are one example of this requirement.)

CONTEXT

- Clarify the context and environments the product will be used in. Consider times, places, and situations beyond "ideal" scenarios. Will sounds compete with traffic or other environmental noises, or will they be used in a contained space with no interference? Will a previously stationary product be used in a mobile context?

- What time of day will the product be used? Are there times when a sound might be annoying to the user?

- What market is this product for? EU only? North America? Global? Does this market require new or existing market or demographic research? Were any previous studies done regarding sound preference for the expected user?

- How might people with different abilities use the product? Use the free, downloadable Microsoft Inclusive Design Toolkit[1] to test product development assumptions, as discussed in Chapter 11.

BRAND QUESTIONS

- Is this a single asset, such as a sound trademark, or a system?

- Are there guidelines for the use of sound and brand? Clarify the scope of the deliverables and their association with brand guidelines.

- Will the "on" sound be used as a sound trademark?

- What, if any, are the current identifiers of the brand? How does this product reflect those brand identifiers?

- What existing sound identity or information systems (if any) will the sound trademark live with?

- How is the product positioned (e.g., entry-level, for kids, professional, medical)? How will the product soundscape reflect this positioning?

COMPETITIVE LANDSCAPE

- What does the competitive landscape of the brand look like? Who uses sounds, and why? Are the sounds loved or hated?

- Does the competition have a product that uses sound as part of its branding strategy? Does the sound associated with the product reflect the brand?

- Do your competitors use too much sound, or sounds that are too loud or too long?

---

1 Albert Shum et al., "Inclusive Microsoft Design," *http://bit.ly/2CrYBgu*.

- Does the sound fit the interaction or use case? What are your competitors doing exceptionally well, and what can be learned from these concepts? Where do they lack, and what can be learned there?

Conclusion

Interviewing is important for understanding what's possible in a project. It should help you understand who is responsible for different aspects, and who you might need to work closely with during the design phase. What you learn during the interview process can prevent unknown surprises linked to the overall scope, pricing, and duration of the project.

Interviews should feel like conversations. Your delivery type may be a single design, an entire experience for a product, or a family of auditory experiences. In some cases, you might find that the product needs subtractive sound design for mechanical noise, which could require the aid of a mechanical engineer. Interviews set your work up for the next step of the process, which is design.

In the next chapter, you'll learn how to apply what you learned in the interviews to designing a successful product.

[8]

Design

DESIGN IS THE STAGE where all of the various considerations for a sound are funneled into the needs of a project. It is where you consider the functional result you are aiming to achieve and brainstorm potential solutions. It is where you can develop a signature style and personality. It is also where you need to specify all the components for every stage and interaction, including visuals, sounds, and haptics.

In some cases, starting with a prototype is actually the best way to begin. Instead of designing the whole project conceptually before making a cheap interactive prototype and finding a flaw, jumping in and testing your assumptions and reactions can be the best way to inform your design decisions. Starting with stock sounds can allow you to play around quickly and cheaply to get a better sense of what you want before spending the time to specify style, length, and personality. If you think prototyping might be the place for you to start, go to Chapter 9 before circling back to the design phase.

Elements of Sound

Having a vocabulary of sound elements can help you design in a way that delivers the desired emotional and situational fit for your product. It can also help you talk more about why a sound is the way it is. This section describes some basic building blocks of sound.

Some waveforms can lend an organic feel to the sounds, and others may make the sound set feel more modern. Understanding the types of waveforms and how they work will help you design sounds that provide the intended outcome.

SINE WAVES

You might have heard the sine wave called the fundamental building block of sound. This is because all sounds can be roughly reduced to a combination of sine waves. Multiply one sine wave by another, and you can produce magnificent, shimmering, bell-like sounds. In popular music, sine waves (and triangle waves, discussed shortly) are often placed underneath other waveforms to fill them out and create the subsonic *boom* and *wub* you hear in bass-heavy music.

A "plain" sine wave is the sound produced when you hit a tuning fork, although you can often hear the sound "wobble" back and forth as it hums (Figure 8-1). One way to describe a plain sine wave would be "clean but boring." It is, for listening purposes, just the fundamental tone. If it is low, it will produce a *bwooooo* sound; if it is high-pitched, it will be a smooth, glassy *fweeeee*.

FIGURE 8-1
A sine wave is produced by striking the steel tines of a tuning fork.

Figure 8-2 shows the sine wave from Dr. Martin Luther King Jr.'s 1963 "I Have a Dream" speech.

FIGURE 8-2
"I Have a Dream" speech given by Martin Luther King Jr. during the March on Washington for Jobs and Freedom on August 28, 1963. (Courtesy of *Archive.org*.)

Zooming in on King's speech reveals that each sound is made of small, nonrepeating sine waves.

Many other waveforms in nature, including speech, applause, singing, and instruments, are simply more complicated, "stacked" versions of sine waves (Figure 8-3).

FIGURE 8-3
Striking two tuning forks of different notes at the same time produces a "stacked" sine wave.

TRANSIENTS

Most speech is made up of transients—short, nonrepeating sine waves that can vary in amplitude, shape, and duration. They can also be difficult for speakers to reproduce effectively, because their intense, rapid energy can overwhelm cheaper hardware. Applause could be considered one of the most basic transients. It involves the initial "clap" of the hands together, and some reverberations that trail off after the initial sound (Figure 8-4).

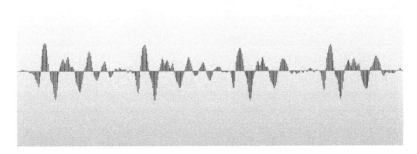

FIGURE 8-4
Zooming in on the noisy applause from King's speech reveals a set of sine waves of different sizes and durations.

For some sounds, the information contained within the transient component makes the sound identifiable. Consider the sound of a single piano note. First, a hammer hits an individual string, and then we hear a vibration that fades over time (Figure 8-5).

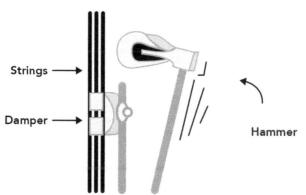

FIGURE 8-5
Piano notes are characterized by an initial burst of high energy as the hammer of the piano hits the string, causing intense vibration.

These initial high-energy bursts are called *onset transients* (Figure 8-6). Without the onset transient, many people cannot identify the sound as a piano. The onset transients are followed by pitch and tonal qualities called *overtones*.

FIGURE 8-6
A single piano note. The onset transient is when the hammer hits the string. The trailing sound consists of diminishing string vibrations.

The vibrations reverberate through the cavity of the piano, amplifying and further shaping the sound—a concept called *cavity resonance* (introduced in Chapter 3) that is especially important with instruments. Pianos of different sizes and shapes interact differently with the vibrations of the strings; for example, a grand piano makes for a deep, rich sound, whereas an upright piano has a smaller, slightly different presence. And although violins and cellos are both string instruments, the size and shape of their cavities and differing length of their strings gives the cello its deep bass presence and the violin its small, sweet resonance.

String instruments are so soulful and emotional because their vibrations contain stacked sine waves, especially when played together. These stacked sine waves create *harmonics*, giving life and the overall tone color of the instrument, to the notes (see Figure 8-7). The vibration of a heavy low note on a cello lasts for a long time, reducing in intensity and expressing many harmonics. The vibration of a violin string, which is shorter and thinner, has its own unique harmonics.

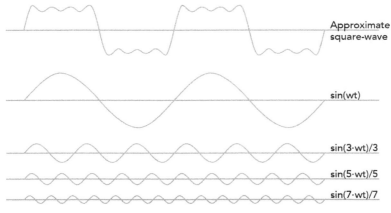

FIGURE 8-7

Stacked versions of sine waves create harmonics, which is what we hear when we listen to vibrations of stringed instruments such as violins. (Source: *http://bit.ly/2Q4bXUe.*)

Sound designers can apply this knowledge to harmonize a computer-generated sound with the cavity resonance of a product, creating a more coherent overall experience. For example, by "tuning" the sounds played inside a product to work in harmony with the cavity resonance, they can make low-quality speakers sound better inside small devices like mobile phones. Adding harmonics to computer-generated sounds in this way can give them life, texture, and meaning.

COMPUTER-GENERATED WAVEFORMS

Pure sine waves—that is, waveforms that create no harmonics—are actually more difficult to create than you might imagine. Before computing resources were cheap and powerful, they were even more difficult to render in the digital domain.

One of the historical advantages of synthetic waves was their cost effectiveness. This is why many products traditionally relied on cheap, computer-generated waves without harmonics, giving us the famous *BEEP BOOP* sounds of early computers.

Synthetic waves, when coupled with other sounds, can provide the building blocks for many interface elements, soundscapes, and alert tones. Working with synthetic waves can be challenging if you want them to sound organic and natural, but the payoff is worth it, as Andy Farnell writes in his book *Designing Sound* (MIT Press): "Although considerable work is required to create synthetic sounds with comparable realism to recordings, the rewards are astonishing. Sounds which are impossible to record become accessible." Some of the tricks that have been used for generating synthetic waves are still useful for low-end markets and for products where affordability is an issue.

SQUARE WAVES

Because they are easy to generate electronically, square waves, shown in Figure 8-8, have long been used as simple electronic alarms and alerts. If you have ever been startled by a particularly harsh, mechanical-sounding beep coming from a piece of hardware, chances are it was a square wave buzzer, probably from a simple piezoelectric synthesizer. The beeping of an old-school Casio wristwatch is a good and somewhat less jarring example.

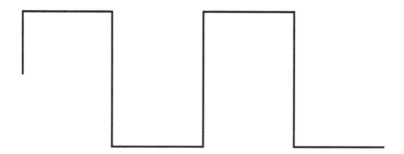

FIGURE 8-8
A square wave.

We often hear square wave alarms because they are cheap to implement, especially in digital logic. Turning a voltage on and off is a binary operation that requires few calculations. If you do this really fast on a device, amplify it, and run it to a speaker, you can make noise for a small amount of money and effort. The 555 integrated circuit, an example of this approach, was invented in 1971 and used in many applications. This simple timer logic chip was one of the most successful chips ever invented,[1] with billions produced since its development.

Outside of alarm clocks, one place you might encounter a square wave is in rock music—specifically, in heavily distorted electric guitars. One of the key effects of a distortion pedal is that it clips the top and bottom off the sine wave, creating something that increasingly resembles a square wave as more distortion is applied. This is one reason why really loud, distorted electric guitars don't just sound like louder guitars, but like a different instrument altogether—hollower, edgier, and angrier.

SAWTOOTH WAVE

A sawtooth wave, shown in Figure 8-9, contains both even and odd harmonics. This richness gives the designer or musician more to work with, especially if they are using filters—there are more harmonics available to shape its sonic character. Sawtooth waves are also easy to generate in both the analog and digital domains.

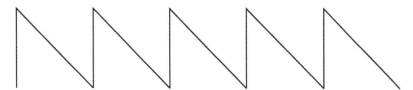

FIGURE 8-9
A simple sawtooth wave.

Sawtooth waves are well known for their use in music. They have been a staple of synthesizers and electric organs since the 1960s. When modified with filters, they can emulate many string, brass, and woodwind instruments. Because they contain both even and odd harmonics,

1 Bill Marsden, "555 Timer Circuits," Lessons in Electric Circuits—Volume VI, *https://www.ibiblio.org/kuphaldt/electricCircuits/Exper/EXP_8.html.*

they're ideal candidates for modification by digital audio filters (consider audio filters a kind of Photoshop for audio), making them popular in electronic music.

RECTANGULAR WAVES

A rectangular wave (Figure 8-10) is essentially a square wave that allows changes in multiple aspects of strength, tone, and pitch. By varying the width of the wave, you can create effects from subtle and interesting to dramatic and disorienting.

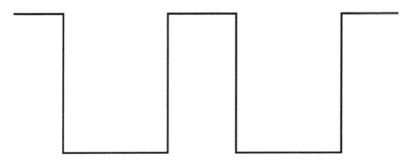

FIGURE 8-10
A rectangular wave

Acoustically, the rectangular wave is often described as having a more "narrow and nasal" sound than a perfect square wave, and its characteristic sound features prominently in many of the big "hollow" bass sounds found in electronic dance music.

PULSE WAVES

A pulse wave, shown in Figure 8-11, is equivalent to a rectangular wave, except the troughs are replaced by silence, creating a repetition of sound pulses. A pulse wave has a "thinner" sound than a rectangular wave and can be used to add different tone colors to sounds.

Pulse Width 50%

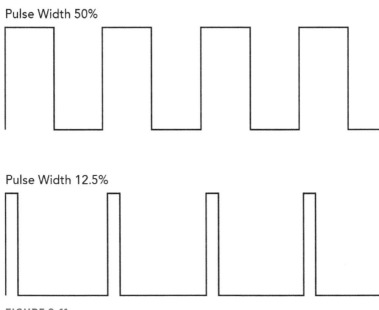

Pulse Width 12.5%

FIGURE 8-11
Pulse waves

A popular use of pulse waves is in the "Hoover" bass sound, where multiple pulse waves are stacked together, an octave apart, and then modulated. Its name derives from the fact that the sound is reminiscent of a vacuum cleaner under load.

TRIANGLE WAVES

One way to think of a triangle wave (Figure 8-12) is that it's a bit like a sawtooth wave with higher frequencies. When you hear "boopy beepy" sounds in films or in music, they are often attributed to triangle waves.

FIGURE 8-12
A triangle wave.

If you need a simple, unobtrusive tone to serve as an audio component, consider a triangle wave. It has more spectral content than a sine wave but less than a sawtooth wave, which can sound harsh without a filter. The triangle wave works great out of the box, so you won't need to modify it too much.

Now that you have a basic understanding of waveforms and how they can be used in creating individual sounds, let's discuss design with respect to overall function and flexibility.

Design to Include the Widest Spectrum of Humanity

[NOTE]

This section, including "Visual to Audio," "Audio to Visual," "Multimodal and Switching Between Senses," and "Different is Normal," was originally published by Kellyn Yvonne Standley and Amber Case on *Medium.com* as "Design for Everybody: How Universal Design Makes Technology Better for All of Us," November 7th, 2018 (*https://medium.com/p/9b5815562b83*).

Creating technology that can be used one-handed, without visual feedback, or without focused attention enables your product to be used more widely, in more circumstances, and under more conditions across the spectrum of humanity. This principle is known as *universal design:* the idea that products, buildings, and environments ought to be created to make them accessible to all people, regardless of age, ability, or other individuating features.

The three senses that most of our technology relies on are sight, hearing, and touch. Being able to convert technological functions fluently between these three senses is an essential skill for the design of interactive technology, spaces, and everyday objects. At times, the intelligent use of different senses means adding lights in place of tones, adding haptics instead of lights, or adding tones in place of spoken language— the key is to develop a fine sensibility for how the interface will work most successfully. The ultimate goal is to allow users to easily develop fluency in interactions with your technology.

Smell, taste, and proprioception, naturally, are far less commonly employed in technology, although proprioception may be gaining steam with the widespread use of virtual reality. Muscle memory can be exceptionally productive to use in some cases—touch typing, for example—because it is the strongest, most durable form of memory, so tasks learned this way can be carried out without conscious attention.

The first stage of design requires determining whether a given function is best carried out by a visual, auditory, or haptic interface. Better yet, each design should allow the user to modify their experience and switch among the three. For digital products, this will allow accessibility to those without sight, without hearing, or without the ability to speak in the programmed language of a voice interface.

When translating between senses, the highest ideal is to create the equivalent experience in another sense rather than mapping the input from one sense directly to the output in another. For example, the performance artist Christine Sun Kim created a "Face Opera," where prelingually deaf performers, including herself at times, create a range of emotive facial expressions in unison, as a chorus; an interpretation of an opera for those who cannot hear music. This is one of the rare creative translations that achieves an analogous experience in a different sense.

There is a place for mapping as well, particularly when a crafted experience is not possible. For instance, text-to-speech applications are key for opening up access to the web for those with vision impairment. But because navigating takes longer when using text-to-speech, conscientious design of websites is still needed to provide access to a simplified navigation menu is important. A quick solution is to simply provide desktop access to a mobile version of the site, as this version likely offers simplified navigation already.

In the following sections, we will discuss converting interfaces and notifications between the three primary senses important to design.

VISUAL TO AUDIO

Consider what translating visual into auditory signals could mean, not simply for people who are blind, but for everyone out there who prefers auditory learning. Sound is far more stimulating to the imagination than visuals. "Radio is like television," some people have quipped, "except the pictures are better."

Where visuals close possibility, sound opens possibility. Sound is not determinative and concrete in the same way visuals are. Was that sound a marble hitting the floor, or was it an almond? (Upon visual inspection, it was, in fact, an almond, although it sounded very much like a marble.) Is that sound rain or bacon frying? Without a visual, few people can tell the difference.

Foley artists create sounds that mimic rain, horses' hooves, and rusty doors, and rarely are these sounds made according to the organic processes that normally produce them. Most people cannot hear the difference because many processes produce similar sounds.

According to various educational centers, roughly 25%–30% of the population state a preference for auditory learning, with about 30% reporting a preference for mixed auditory, visual, and kinesthetic stimulus.[2] Combined, this represents the majority of the population. While there is debate over whether a preferred learning style actually translates into better when it's presented in their preferred medium, researchers find ample evidence in the literature that people express preferences for one form of stimulus over another and that such preferences persist in individuals over time.[3] Because preferences often determine the medium an individual will voluntarily seek out, these preferences are important in directing the development of content. The availability of auditory lessons would allow students to engage with material in different ways, perhaps boosting repetition and thus retention.

The popularity of podcasts may underscore a widespread interest in auditory learning, or a natural spillover of information into a channel of perception that is less overburdened. In 2018, about 44% of Americans reported listening to podcasts at one time or another. Over a quarter of the population—and a full third of those between the ages of 24 and 55—listened to podcasts monthly.[4]

---

2 For more information, see "Learning Style (Auditory, Visual & Kinesthetic) & Dyslexics," Dyslexia Victoria, http://bit.ly/2qieQ8z, and "Auditory Learners," Studying Style, https://www.studyingstyle.com/auditory-learners/.

3 Harold Pashler, Mark McDaniel, Doug Rohrer, and Robert Bjork, "Learning Style, Concepts and Evidence," Psychological Science in the Public Interest 9, no. 3 (2008): 105–119.

4 Edison Research, "The Infinite Dial 2018," https://www.edisonresearch.com/infinite-dial-2018/.

Podcasts have been pioneering auditory teaching and representation of data (sonification) through sound effects. Conveying quantities and proportions is a particularly important challenge because visual formats are quite effective at conveying such information. One radio segment on automated stock trading represents the time it takes to deliver a "sell" order from Chicago ("bup... ... ...bup") versus sending it from the building next to the New York Stock Exchange ("bup-bup") to explain why an arms race of proximity led to new rules to create equality among different trading firms. Podcasts are rich sources of creative ideas for representing information with sound.

Text-to-speech for websites can use similar methods. For example, using long tones to represent increments of 10 and short tones to represent increments of 1 allows a listener to "hear" the proportions of different elements of a pie chart or a graph.

Partnering with an inclusive design team, the University of Colorado is working to develop a purely auditory version of its online lessons in physics. The purpose is not to simply read aloud the text of the lessons, but to convey an understanding of the concepts in a separate, unique fashion solely with sound. Instead of learning of the Bohr radius through an image, what would it be like to hear it in sound?

More difficult is translating rich visual information to sound. *Soundscape* is a smartphone app that uses binaural audio combined with local information to guide the blind as they walk around their neighborhoods. It can identify landmarks and streets, and guide users to locations using sound cues. Might this be modified for tourists exploring new cities, where a verbal guide is reassuring?

Pushing the idea further, we now have access to high-quality sound through microspeakers that could be placed in complex patterns on a wall or ceiling.[5] Would it be possible to "paint with sound" to convey an abstract image in greater detail? Could we really begin to "feel" the shape and texture of the art if we expressed the sound in enough individual detail?

---

[5] Robert Miles, "Micro Speakers Market, Size, Growth Drivers, Market Opportunities, Industry Trends and Forecast to 2021," IDA Repor, *http://bit.ly/2SsfNIr*.

What about translating language to sound and music? We make cashiers memorize dozens of numerical codes, though few would report this as a skill they excel at. Music, on the other hand, is something we memorize almost without effort when it is distinctive and heard regularly. What if instead of making announcements over a loudspeaker, we assigned musical phrases to common communications between employees, much like the African talking drum mentioned in Chapter 3?

A new system of musical sounds would aim for something short of Morse code, with its near infinite combinations, but would be able to communicate at least a few dozen individual, unique messages.

AUDIO TO VISUAL

Because sound is an excellent way to maintain ambient awareness, some groups are making efforts to translate sound into visuals for those with hearing impairment, often including icons to indicate the sound's likely source—a human male or female, a child, a car alarm, and so on.

Such efforts are genuinely challenging. Music, for example, can feature not only a melody, but also harmonic and inharmonic overtones, percussive sounds, horns and trumpets, piano played softly or *forte*, sampled birdsong, human voice, and on and on. As Rainier Plomp notes in *The Intelligent Ear*, "In everyday life, we are usually surrounded by many sound sources...the ear is able to disentangle these vibrations so faithfully that we are not aware of the fact that they were ever mixed."[6] Our ears translate one singular complex waveform—picked up by our eardrums—to represent many different sounds, instruments, and sources. How can any visualization convey as much information? Most visualizations are created to add a pleasant visual experience to music, not to genuinely translate auditory information into an equivalent visual and haptic experience.

The experience of music and sound is emotive. It is unlikely that, even if all the information were present in visual and haptic forms, the result would create the same emotional experience. This is why Christine Sun Kim's "Face Opera" is such an ingenious approach: it directly cues into the viewer's feelings and creates an analogous experience, just through other means.

---

6   Reinier Plomp, *The Intelligent Ear: On the Nature of Sound Perception* (London: Lawrence Erlbaum Associates, 2002), 1. For those interested, *The Intelligent Ear* is an excellent discussion of how our understanding of sound has evolved from an imprecise approximation in scientific equations to a more realistic and messy picture of sound.

Curiously, music does not evoke all the emotions we experience in daily life, and this is perhaps the most important aspect of the experience of music. Although music can evoke anger, it cannot evoke either contempt or jealousy. There have been many attempts to explain the way that music evokes emotions, and to relate them to pitch, tempo, tone color, major and minor chords, and other aspects of music.[7] Yet the only observation that seems to hold universally with music is this one about the limited range of emotions music evokes—perhaps the strongest argument in favor of the idea that some emotions are not, in fact, natural to human beings, and that one day we may move past them. "People must learn to hate," Nelson Mandela said, "and if they can learn to hate, they can be taught to love. For love comes more naturally to the human heart than its opposite." This may explain why people fall in love with music, and follow it throughout their lives.

Perhaps the reason people feel connected with the crowd at a live concert is that the experience of music creates a unique state where we can connect with each other freely and comfortably, without the emotions that divide us. This, unfortunately, is an experience that the "Face Opera" cannot capture. In his book *Musicophilia*, Oliver Sacks describes patients with musical afflictions, from musical auras with epilepsy to a continuous flow of spontaneous musical inspiration after a near-death experience. Perhaps someday, we will be able to directly induce the spontaneous experience of music in our brains, and of the deaf will be able to experience it. One patient in *Musicophilia* notes:

> I do have fragments of poetry and sudden phrases darting into my mind, but with nothing like the richness and range of my spontaneous musical imagery. Perhaps it is not just the nervous system, but music itself that has something very peculiar about it—its beat, its melodic contours, so different from those of speech, and its peculiarly direct connection to the emotions. It really is a very odd business that all of us, to varying degrees, have music in our heads.[8]

7 Marjolein van der Zwaag, Joyce Westerink, and Egon van den Broek, "Emotional and Psychophysiological Responses to Tempo, Mode, and Percussiveness," *Musicae Scientiae* 15 no. 2 (2011): 250–269.

8 Oliver Sacks, *Musicophilia: Tales of Music and the Brain* (New York: Alfred A. Knopf, 2007), 40.

There are promising avenues using visualizations to convey sound with less than a complete capture of all the information present. The most direct way to visualize sound is the Schlieren method, which uses a setup of mirrors and lenses to capture the compression of air molecules with sound or heat. Like watching minuscule ripples in water, sound and heat waves appear like light and dark waves emanating from around the source. Real-time visualizations based on this aesthetic could be both interesting and informative.

In the realm of notifications, LED strips or panels can be used for visual directions in the event of an emergency, lighting up the most important information and directing people along the most efficient path.

For the hearing impaired, bursts of colors on a smartphone paired with haptics could indicate the type of notification, much like distinctive sounds indicate the nature of notifications for those with hearing. Phones could come with optional settings so those who desired could turn on an option for "visualized sound" to translate audio notifications into visuals.

VISUAL AND AUDIO TO HAPTIC

Haptics are underutilized in terms of their versatility. It is worthwhile to consider more sophisticated ways to pair haptic stimuli with sound or visuals, using rhythm and a wider array of haptic sensations. For electronic devices, play with different haptic motors to create distinctive vibration patterns. When paired with audio and visual, these subtle haptics can create a truly immersive experience.

Haptics are a promising avenue to explore as a more natural replacement for the ambient awareness created by sound. Unlike visuals, they do not require our primary attention, or for us to be looking in any particular direction. The mesh of sensors in the Teslasuit, for example, which was developed for gaming (like most haptic suits), can convey not only sensations of touch, including the sensation of wind or water, but also of hot and cold. If coded instead to convey sounds picked up in the environment, haptic suits could provide an intuitive ambient awareness for different senses. Haptic compass belts provide accessible wearable options, as they can be easily looped around the waist. The belts contain multiple buzzers that are programmed to buzz in the direction of north.

MULTIMODAL AND SWITCHING BETWEEN SENSES

More and more, our devices will use all three of these senses (sight, hearing, and touch), and the main task will be finding intelligent roles for each. Language can require too much concentrated attention at times, and sound can be intrusive. Often, spoken commands can be converted to tones, and tones can often be converted to lights or haptics. Be creative. We may find that many of our user interfaces are more complex than they need to be, and simpler solutions work better. Instead of driving directions being conveyed exclusively in spoken language, perhaps tones could help indicate the distance to an approaching turn. The direction of the turn could be indicated by a vibration in your seat—a vibration on the left meaning turn left and a vibration on the right meaning turn right. Although the street names would likely need to remain spoken, the direction of turns could be more seamlessly intuitive if integrated into physical sensations, and tones may be a more discreet reminder of the distance to an upcoming turn.

There is likely to be an increasing emphasis on optionality in future devices. Being able to convert notifications between senses allows us to customize our experience for a broader range of contexts. On websites, it would be advantageous if the display could be converted to different themes adjusted for those with color-blindness (for whom certain colors, like red will not be easily distinguishable), those who need larger text, or higher contrast (which can also be useful when using a laptop outside with the glare of sunlight), or converted to audible text along with sonification for data or images. With the game-changing BLITAB Braille tablet,[9] it is increasingly likely that the internet will open up for the blind and visually impaired as never before.

DIFFERENT IS NORMAL

By widening our understanding of who can be helped by technology, we can open up the work of design to conquer new challenges. In a survey about technology use that included difficulties due to any cause, including arthritis, dyslexia, and any other limitation, only 21% of working-age adults reported being entirely free from challenges in

---

9   For more information, check out their website, *http://www.blitab.com.*

working with technology.[10] Our concepts of "disability" and "fully able" have been misleading us. Most of us struggle with technology in one way or another.

Luckily, difficulty exposes fruitful areas for new products and new approaches, and innovation that solves a niche problem often helps all of us. Pots and pans made for arthritic customers, designed to balance easily when lifted from the stove, also reduce the risk of spills for "fully able" people by making them easier to handle proficiently.[11] Ferrari designed the Enzo with subtly roomier seats and bigger doors to spare the knees of aging pensioners, and these changes also make it easier for the rest of us to get in and out without bumps and bruises, even if we are capable of navigating ordinary car doors most of the time. Wider tolerances simply mean technology works successfully more of the time.

Frequently, identifying the ideal group for testing can be a highly effective way of discovering novel information about the effectiveness of your design. This is true even when this group does not represent the main population of intended users. Knives developed to meet the demands of the busiest of chefs result in better longevity, a more precise grip, and better balance for casual cooks who are simply using them in their own kitchens. Using blind testers for self-driving cars rapidly identifies points of friction in the interface, allowing these to be refined and eliminated for all users.[12]

Designing to a limitation offers a tool for injecting creativity and variation into design processes that have stalled. Creativity loves constraint. When given the freedom to explore new avenues, there is virtually nothing more stimulating to the design process.

Variation is often in low supply, as corporate cultures tend to promote safe affirmations of conventions over bold ventures in new directions. In *Drive: The Surprising Truth About What Motivates Us* (Riverhead Books), Daniel Pink highlights research, demonstrating that extrinsic

---

10 Forrester Research, "The Wide Range of Abilities and Its Impact on Computer Technology," Study Commissioned by Microsoft, *http://bit.ly/2JmvVXD*.

11 For example, the pots and pans created by Factory Design, the winner of the DBA Inclusive Design Challenge in 2003.

12 See Bruel Allman-Ward and Kjaer Allman-Ward, "'Robot, Take Me to the Pub!' Sound Design for Future Electric/Autonomous Vehicles," Engineering Integrity Society, *http://bit.ly/2zsdyfi*.

motivators—such as money and approval—are actually inhibitors to creative thinking, including problem solving and other forms of knowledge work. These motivators are quite effective for physical and rote work—the kinds that made up the bulk of work for most of human history—but creative tasks, which are set to dominate the economy after automation comes of age, are far better driven by intrinsic motivation, such as a personal challenge, curiosity, a desire for knowledge, or altruistic motivations to create something.

For an example of designing to a limitation, an architect was hired to design the blueprints for a house for someone who had lost three limbs, including both legs and one arm, with the aim of creating suitable accommodations. The result was simply a gentler and more accommodating space. It features lower rises on the stairs; two shower heads, one with a raised platform appropriate for someone sitting, or for the owner when he is not wearing his prosthetic legs; ample attention to the height of appliances, drawers, countertops, and more. Similar adaptations and attention can make housing more comfortable for others as well. Designing for a specific person or group allows conventions to be reevaluated and variation introduced. This is essential to allow for selection based on preference, and this selection process is key for the evolution of technology.

In many ways, the ubiquity of limitation is good news for design. In his book *Change by Design*, Tim Brown points out that we're frequently so accustomed to compensating for the deficiencies in the technology we already have that it is difficult for us to imagine a form of technology that would be better adapted to us.[13]

Bee Wilson gives an example:

> Food in cans was invented long before it could easily be used. A patent for Nicolas Appert's revolutionary new canning process was issued in 1812, and the first canning factory opened in Bermondsey, London, in 1813. But it would be another fifty years before anyone managed to devise a can opener.[14]

---

13 Tim Brown, *Change by Design* (New York: HarperCollins, 2009).

14 Bee Wilson, *Consider the Fork: A History of How We Cook and Eat* (New York: Basic Books, 2012).

In the early decades, tin cans needed to be hammered open. A more modern, thin tin can was invented in 1846. This was then followed by can openers and self-opening cans, like sardine tins. We simply cannot know that we are missing a technology until it is invented, and until then, we simply make do.

What developed, technology should be appropriated into new, positive creative uses. Yet stigma often prevents the spread of information between groups and among the general public when a product is associated with disability. Color-blind artists can use the smartphone app Visual AI in order to identify colors accurately, even though it was originally developed for the blind. Yet because we do not talk about disability freely, these artists may not know it exists. Companies can do good in the world and increase the size and creativity of their markets by helping to eradicate stigma against disability. After all, this is where much innovation is set to occur in the decades to come.

Even if your products do not target users with specific limitations, they will be more innovative, more integrated, and more seamless if you develop them in communication with a test audience that places high demands on your device or interface. Universal design is no longer a choice; it is a part of good design.

Creating a Design Document

Once you have settled on the way you will handle individual interactions, the next step is to specify what you are going to create. A design document plots out every auditory component of a device, including alerts, playback, and any sounds that occur in the course of normal operation. It also includes the coordinated haptics and visuals that accompany each state of the device and the desired connotation you would like the customer to infer from the sound. A mood board is often included to demonstrate the overall aesthetics of the project, as we will describe later in this chapter. If you are working with a sound engineer, a good design document makes it easier for them to create sounds that fit your vision.

BUILD AN AUDIO MAP

The audio map is where you map out all product states, sound types, and the duration of each sound:

- Audio response, type, and length

- Light response, type, and length

- Haptic response, type, and length

An audio map has two roles: to provide information valuable to the understanding and use of a device, and to contribute to the product identity, which is part of the brand behind it. If it is an existing product, you'll need two maps: a map of the current product states, and a new map with the desired changes.

When creating a new set of sounds, start with the *connotation*, or implication, you would like the customer to take from the sound. This connotation is a well-defined goal to aim for—a target for when your interaction is successful. For instance, it is common to desire a "power off" sound to connote "resolution." Focusing on the connotation is important when you are adapting products for new demographics and foreign markets. If you move to a different market, you can test the user experience against the desired connotation and know what you need to change to create the same meaning for your new demographic. Consider what personalities will be inferred, and what personality you want.

When specifying a sound, you will also want to describe the overall style you are aiming for. The terms in Table 5-1 may be useful.

The example shown in Table 8-1 and Figure 8-13 is for Samsung's 2017 *Star Wars*–themed POWERbot robotic vacuum cleaner. To create an audio map, break up the interactions into functions. This example only pairs states with sounds, and each sound has a specific reference already, so describing the sound in terms of connotations and style is not necessary in this case. For both reasons, it is simpler than mapping a device that uses lights, haptics, and new sounds to be developed.

TABLE 8-1. Example audio map for Samsung's POWERbot robotic vacuum

ACTION STATES	
Power on	Lightsaber sound
Power off	Lightsaber sound
Start	Breathing sound
Stop (pause)	Breathing sound
Start clean after stop (pause)	Breathing sound
Normal mode	Breathing sound and "The Imperial March (Darth Vader's Theme)"
Switch to Turbo mode	"You are powerful!"
Switch to Normal mode	"Good"
Switch to Quiet mode	No sound
Start spot clean	Breathing sound
Finish spot clean	Breathing sound
Return to charger	"The Imperial March (Darth Vader's Theme)"
STATUS STATES	
Start charging	Breathing sound
Charging complete	Breathing sound
Successfully returned to charger	"Impressive"
Can't return to charger	Stun blaster sound
Vacuum stuck	Stun blaster sound
PROGRAMMING STATES	
Manual clean mode	Breathing sound (at different times), "Impressive," "Good"
Allow/block smart control	Breathing sound
Turn on repeat clean mode	"There will be no one to stop us now"
Turn off repeat clean mode	Breathing sound
Restart cleaning when charging is complete	Breathing sound
Enter settings	Breathing sound
Complete settings	Breathing sound
Cancel settings	"No"
Set current time	Breathing sound

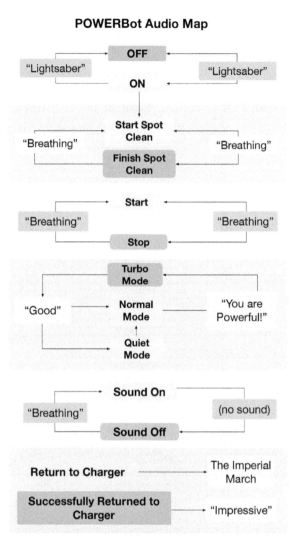

POWERBot Audio Map

FIGURE 8-13

A slightly simplified
audio map of the
Star Wars-themed
POWERbot.

The next section will cover the creation of a deliverable table.

CREATE A DELIVERABLE TABLE

When you're building a sound set, it is useful to organize what needs to
be created in a deliverable table or list. A deliverable table is a quick way
of determining and tracking the deliverables needed for the project.
This is different from a product map or a design document, because it
simply outlines the sounds needed for the final product.

During the development of a product, we may discover or suggest different use cases for a particular sound. A *use case* is a list of actions or steps that define the interactions to achieve a particular goal. Defining use cases can be as simple as saying, "We need a sound for when the doorbell rings" or as complex as a hundred pages of wireframes that describe how sound can support the interaction or the experience as a whole. At this point you need to make decisions and define what you will design for—the interactions that require sound to be added, changed, or removed.

Once you have made this list, you can integrate it into your deliverable table, as shown in Table 8-2. This simple table specifies the types of sounds you are looking for and pairs them with the individual states of a device. Making a table of the sounds, lights, and haptics of a device is useful, because it takes your mental picture and makes it shareable. You'll be able to expand this table into a design document and during prototyping and testing you'll use it to determine what fits and what doesn't, what states might make more sense, and what senses are overwhelmed or missing. The deliverable table clarifies designers' thinking by having them map out all sound, haptic, and visual states.

TABLE 8-2. A sample set of deliverables for a device-based mobile product. Depending on the project, there are many different categories you can use in your matrix. We recommend starting with something simple like this.

USE CASE	FILENAME	USE CASE DESCRIPTION: WHAT THE USER HEARS WHEN...	FREQUENCY OF OCCURRENCE	STYLE
App start	*startup.wav*	...they launch the app	Seldom; app usually remains open <1 week	Timbral
Alert/ warning	*warning.wav*	...they are about to do something that can't be undone	Seldom; this is an infrequent case	Rhythmic
New message	*newmessage.wav*	...a new text message is available	Often	Timbral
Incoming voice call	*ringtone.wav*	...someone is calling	Often	Timbral, melodic

Identify the most likely use cases and events, and group them into the classes and categories that fit best. Set lengths for each sound and the interactions associated with the product.

As the project progresses, you can consult the deliverable table as a master reference for implementation. Keep it up to date and easily viewable by project participants.

DEVELOP DESIGN ELEMENTS

Next, we offer advice for how to develop your creative vision for the project, how to add variety, and how to ensure that your sounds work on a range of playout hardware. This step will also allow you to specify your sounds with greater detail in your design document.

Create a mood board

A mood board is a collection of elements that can inspire the aesthetics of a project. They are a good way to communicate hard-to-describe aesthetics and emotions, and building them is an easy and fun task. The elements can be visual, or they can be a collection of sounds or samples from songs, or even three-dimensional objects. Finding your aesthetic style through association with different mood elements is one of the fastest ways to get moving on a sound design project. To get started, you can take cues from the visual interface, materials, and existing soundscapes and cultures associated with the product.

Mood boards work well when adjectives (smooth, shiny, expensive, organic) are used to communicate ideas about sound.

Consider the visual interface

If the product has a visual interface, you can take cues from what that interface already communicates. Is the visual interface serious and clinical? You might want to develop a soundscape that matches the mood. If the interface looks like a retro video game, you can take cues from that existing soundscape. A visual interface that is minimal and futuristic might have minimal, futuristic sounds. Working with what's already there is a good place to start.

Consider the product's materials and textures

The clues for what the product should sound like are in the physical materials that compose it (see Figure 8-14). Conversely, if the product has not yet been defined and the materials haven't been chosen, your soundscape might help determine what the product could look like.

FIGURE 8-14
Examples of different textures and materials. How might you design a soundscape for a product that is based on the texture of each material?

One approach to branded sound design is to map traditional brand attributes to aspects of the sound. Creative mapping has saved many good designs that might otherwise struggle for client buy-in.

Consider different soundscapes and cultures

Our cultural interpretation of a specific soundscape is often just as individual as people themselves. Depending on your background—such as being part of a generation that played video games, or growing up in a culture with a different tonal scale—you are going to interpret sounds differently. For instance, an industrial worker might interpret mechanical sounds differently than a software engineer that grew up with video games.

Add variety

Don't just think about what sound is played at what time, but consider adding a variety of sounds to some state changes, especially if they are repetitive. A voice interface will get repetitive if it says only a few things. In the POWERbot's "manual clean" mode, the Darth Vader breathing sound is followed by a varied reply of "impressive" or "good." This is a reasonable way to add interest, personality, and surprise to robotic interaction systems.

If you're looking to determine, design, or test sounds when the product hasn't been built yet, consider using animation to demonstrate product states, flows, and associated sounds, and build them directly from an audio map as a reference.

Design for those with different sensory needs

Many people have sensitivities to certain types of sensory stimulation. Autistic individuals in particular get easily overwhelmed by light, sound, vibration, and other stimuli. It's important for products, services, and spaces to accommodate users with such sensitivities in their designs. In the United States, for example, AMC Theaters provides a sensory-friendly option for moviegoers. The theaters include low-level lighting and reduced sound. They allow talking, the presence of caregivers, and outside snacks for viewers with restricted diets.

To help ensure your devices can be used by those with different sensory needs, build in an option to turn sound down or eliminate it entirely.

Check that the sound works at a variety of resolutions

Just like images, audio should be recognizable at high and low resolution. It's important to be able to hear sound trademarks and audio-based notifications across the many different contexts in which they're played (Figure 8-15). For example, sonic logos are sometimes used across media—radio, advertising, TV—and also are potentially embedded in products. Make sure the logo plays well at low quality; see how well it degrades. Some devices are mobile, and others are fixed; some devices will be located in loud environments and break through background noise, and others will be in quieter, more sensitive spaces. Test in a variety of contexts.

If you're designing for a range of hardware, consider creating a sound set with fuller, deeper sounds for higher-quality hardware, and less rich, more computer-generated sounds for lower-quality hardware—but keep the experience of the brand coherent. An acoustic version of a digital logo will sound good when played on nice surround-sound speakers, and a low-resolution, simplified sound set could be played on lower-quality mobile hardware.

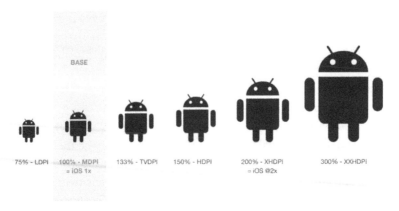

FIGURE 8-15

Just like visual logos, audio logos should be recognizable on different playout hardware.

Shape the soundscape personality

Create your initial soundscape using your desired connotations for the sounds, and then shape the result into the type of personality you would like to see come through. Regardless of whether you intend it or not, people will infer a personality from the sounds your product makes. This is discussed with respect to voice user interfaces in Chapter 6.

Interaction Checklist

Here is a simple sound design checklist to ensure your design document includes all relevant information. Make sure the intention of each interaction is clear.

PURPOSE

- What is the purpose of the sound?
- Evaluate: Is sound necessary for this interaction?

TRIGGER

- What event makes the sound happen?
- Is the sound affiliated with an image or animation?

INFORMATION

- What information does the sound convey?
- Match the sound to the relative urgency or nonurgency of the information

LOCATION

- Where is the product likely to be relative to the user when it plays the sound?
- How does the sound play in different environments?
- Is the product likely to be in a pocket or purse when it is carried?

MISSED NOTIFICATION

- What happens if the user misses the audio notification?
- Is there a backup that can convey the information in a different sense?
- Can a haptic element decrease the likelihood of a notification being missed, and is this useful?

CONTEXT

- Could this sound interrupt people nearby?
- Could this sound be played at an inappropriate time? If so, when?
- Have you tested the durability of the sounds by playing them many times over the course of the day?

INCLUSIVITY

- Does the sound work for individuals with temporarily or permanently blocked senses?
- Can the alert be delivered in a different way to ensure the message is correctly received?
- Does the product work for a variety of people, not just those in the test demographic?
- Have you provided a way to turn the sound up, down, or off, or change the sound?

CONTEXTUAL TESTING

- Does your product work in a variety of contexts?

- Do you need to add any additional settings to allow the user to match the experience to the environment and social context they are in?

If your design process addresses all of these considerations, you will be in good shape. Make sure that relevant information is conveyed in your design brief, which will carry your visual aesthetic, your product's audio map, the deliverable table for each sound you are developing with its style, connotation, and length, and discussions of how you would like the experience of each interaction to go. As sounds are completed, they can be checked off the deliverable table; changes to the design of the interaction and changing visual to sound or haptic cues can be tracked in the master document.

Conclusion

Having a vocabulary of sound elements can help communicate the shape of the deliverables to multiple participants in the project. Knowing about various kinds of waves, transients, and their uses in design can help shape specific sounds towards desired effects. Considering how sounds might be changed into different senses, or how different situations and human differences might affect product interactions is another important aspect of the design process.

Creating a design document will help organize important details, nuances, and considerations during the design process. In addition to an audio map, this document serves as a portable, trackable guide that can be shared across clients, user experience and sound designers, allowing everyone to keep tabs of what's done and what needs more work. You'll use the design process to create a series of prototypes, which we'll discuss in the next chapter. The prototypes will be essential to the user testing process, as they will allow design directions to be tested and modified. The interview, design, prototype, user experience and hardware testing cycle may be repeated multiple times during longer projects—or during projects that take more time to find their footing—and it may be visited again during product updates many years in the future.

[9]

Prototyping

DESIGNING SOUND IS A process that involves selling something invisible. You may need to use your imagination and give yourself and others the opportunity to compare their expectations with what you've created. This approach allows you to make suggestions in a streamlined way without so much explanation. A good prototype tells its own story.

Prototyping and testing assumptions early and often is important but is often overlooked by upper management. One demonstration of this comes from the marshmallow spaghetti tower challenge, an exercise that asks small groups to work together to build the tallest spaghetti structure strong enough to support the weight of a marshmallow. Studies on these sessions have proven that kindergarteners consistently build better structures than CEOs.[1] The reason? Kindergarteners tested their structures often to see if they bore the weight of the marshmallow, while CEOs waited until the building phase was completed before adding the marshmallow, only then discovering their structure did not survive the stress.

There are several stages at which you can test the quality, reaction to, and feasibility of sounds. The first stage is before the product is built. You can listen to a set of sounds with an interactive palette. You can mock up the product with paper prototypes, animations, or audio-only prototypes with contextual sounds. You can use existing products and overlay the considered sounds using the magic of video.

The second stage is when the device is prototyped. You can play the sounds now with some sense of the final shape, materials, and play-out hardware of the product. When you have the device prototyped you

---

1 Maren Hedrich, "What 20 sticks of spaghetti and one single marshmallow taught us about innovation," proxyclick, *http://bit.ly/2JN8EOO*.

can create videos, contextual prototypes, and recordings of the product being used in context. You can also use these prototypes to swap out sounds. This stage might also benefit from a video with sound overlaid.

The final stage is when the device is nearly complete and you have a solid understanding of all aspects of the product. You might not be able to control or access speakers in your office. To solve this, consider bringing your own speakers, audio converters, and playable interfaces. This process can be quite complex, or it can be simple, especially if you are building on a sound that already exists. Broadly speaking, you have three options for sourcing sounds:

- You can use a *stock sound* from a library.

- You can sample and edit an *existing sound* from the real world.

- You can *synthesize a sound*, either directly or by writing code that synthesizes and controls it (as with generative audio).

In many cases, your best approach might be to combine two or more of these options, mixing them as appropriate within your overall sound set, or even within a single sound instance. We will focus on stock sounds and sound libraries to help you get started.

Stock Sounds and Sound Libraries

A stock sound is simply a sound that someone else has recorded and optimized, then made available for use by others. Stock sounds are usually clustered into sound libraries, of which there are literally thousands—some paid, and some free to use. Stock sounds can be useful for prototyping, but they can sound tacky if they're not modified, or if they do not come from a good source. Be sure to look for sounds at the highest resolution possible, or you lose quality.

ADVANTAGES

The biggest advantage of using a stock sound is its economy, both in money and in time. Once you have familiarized yourself with a few libraries and secured a small budget to license sounds (or accepted the limitations that come with free libraries), bringing a sound into your project can be a matter of spending a few minutes searching. This makes stock sound an excellent option for projects with short deadlines and no time to record and edit. Libraries also make it possible to throw together a reasonably convincing audio user interface on a tight budget.

Stock sounds are also useful when you are out of ideas. Just as a fashion designer might wander through a fabric store for inspiration, sound designers sometimes work through a creative dry spell by listening to stock recordings and imagining how they might fit into a current project.

And because stock sounds are essentially "disposable," they are excellent for uncertain situations, such as creating a quick prototype, or working with a client whose vision is poorly defined or subject to frequent shifts. This also makes stock sounds a good choice when you're working with a new client who is risk-averse and wants to go with sounds that are familiar or stereotypical.

DISADVANTAGES

The biggest disadvantage of stock sounds is that many are so widely used that they can be recognizable. Off-the-shelf samples, often the same ones over and over, are used in films. If a cat meows and hisses in a movie, it is frequently the same sample as the last one you heard in a different movie (although the untrained ear frequently does not notice the repetition). As another example, a helicopter starting up or landing is typically the sound of a Bell Hughes 47G from the 1950s— despite the fact that modern helicopters sound very different. "[In film] every helicopter shutting down emits the chirp-chirp-chirp sound of the rubber drive belts disengaging," explains the Clichés section of FilmSound.org, "in spite of the fact that only the famous Bell 47G (the *MASH* chopper) actually makes this sound."[2]

So if you are using a stock sound, you should make an effort to alter it in some way. Altering the sound will allow it to fit your context more precisely and keep it from sounding too familiar to users. You can often achieve this by splitting up the sample and reconstructing it, modifying the tone, or creating a new sound using the original one as inspiration.

If you are creating a unique hardware or software product, on the other hand, you probably should not be using stock sounds. At worst, your product's sounds might conflict with a different product's sounds and your customers will not be able to tell the difference!

---

2 "Film Sound Cliches," FilmSound.org, *http://www.filmsound.org/cliche/*.

TYPES OF SOUND LIBRARIES AND COPYRIGHT LICENSING

The first issue to contend with when using stock sounds is licensing, or the terms by which you are permitted to use copyrighted material. Recording your own audio from nature gives you unlimited rights to use that sound any way you like, but with stock sound libraries permissions are a little more complicated.

There are three main kinds of sound libraries, each of which has different usage guidelines.

Free libraries

The first category comprises public domain libraries. These are completely free to use and do not need to be credited, even for commercial use. A couple of the better-known sites include:

The Hollywood Edge (https://hollywoodedge.com)
> 520,000 sound effects available for your productions

Film Sound Effects (http://fselibrary.com)
> A historic sound library with sounds from 1966 (recorded on digital audio tape, or DAT), now redigitized at 24-bit 48K Mono BWAV

Each resource has its own focus, quirks, and flavor, so do some digging before committing to one. Think of using sound samples as you would using stock textures or photos.

Creative Commons sound libraries

The second type of library has a Creative Commons license, which essentially makes it free to use, but with certain defined limitations. It is important to check which kind of Creative Commons license a stock sound uses. Some licenses are for commercial use and simply require an attribution somewhere in the product. Others do not allow commercial use at all and are for creative projects only. When in doubt, contact the creator of the sound or the website where you found the sound. Examples in this category include:

FreeSound (https://freesound.org)
> A collaborative database of Creative Commons sounds

SoundBible (http://soundbible.com)
> Thousands of free sound effects, sound clips, and straight-up sounds, both Creative Commons and commercially licensable.

Professional sample or sound effect libraries

Finally, there are many—often more expensive—professional sample or sound effect libraries. These are nice because they are set up as professional services, meaning the quality of the samples is uniformly high, they are organized in a logical and searchable way, and they come with legitimate customer support. If you are going to be sampling a lot, and time is money, they are often worth the expense. Most professional sound libraries work on a subscription model in which you pay a set amount per month or year for access, and are free to use the contents without citing the source. As long as you adhere to the laws around copyrighted media, you can sample what you like.

Prototype Delivery Formats

Once you've sourced your sounds, but before completing work on your product, you'll want to deliver your sounds in a way that the client can hear and review them. Depending on the project, you might choose from a variety of methods. This section discusses some commonly used formats that are easy for clients to play with, respond to, and understand.

INTERACTIVE PALETTES

An *interactive palette* is an audio-only prototype of the interaction. It is useful for mapping out sounds at the preproduct stage. If a mood board gives impressions, a palette organizes those impressions into concepts. This is one step beyond an initial playable prototype, because it incorporates the feedback from the initial stages of your sound design ideas.

An interactive palette provides stakeholders with a clickable interface to try out sounds grouped by categories such as mood, material type, and design direction. Playing with these interactive presentation tools gives stakeholders a sense of agency and control. After comparing options, they can make their choice by physically selecting (via mouse or touch) the sound they want. Figures 9-1 and 9-2 show some examples of interactive palettes.

Sound Demo Interactive Palette

	Power On	Power Off	Notification
Minimal	Sound A	Sound A	Sound A
	Sound B	Sound B	Sound B
	Sound C	Sound C	Sound C
Modern	Sound A	Sound A	Sound A
	Sound B	Sound B	Sound B
	Sound C	Sound C	Sound C
Familiar	Sound A	Sound A	Sound A
	Sound B	Sound B	Sound B
	Sound C	Sound C	Sound C

FIGURE 9-1

A clickable interface featuring three different sound palettes. This table format allows clients to easily explore and experience sounds from a single page instead of playing them from a folder.

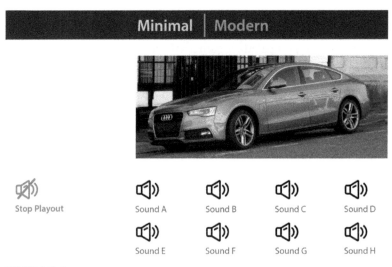

Minimal | Modern

Stop Playout

Sound A Sound B Sound C Sound D

Sound E Sound F Sound G Sound H

FIGURE 9-2

A clickable interface for car sounds for a major vehicle manufacturer in the 2000s. This format includes audio embedded in a web page, and can be played on a laptop or tablet device. This two-tabbed interface contains sets of Minimal and Modern themed sound examples for the client to choose from.

VIDEO WITH SOUND OVERLAY

A lot of what goes into designing products with sound is making a coherent package containing the haptics, the lights, the interface, and the sounds themselves. This is where a video of an interaction within the appropriate context can help give you a genuine sense of what works and what doesn't.

If you have an existing product that you are evaluating for new sounds, or a prototype of one, you can simply record a user interacting with the actual device and edit the audio track to present different sound options.

For example, let's say you are hired to evaluate the sounds on an electric kettle. The most cost-effective intervention is to simply reduce the volume on the tone that plays when the kettle is set. A simple video of a user setting the kettle to boil and returning to pour the hot water in to a teacup after the second tone is an effective way demonstrate the different sound options, including the reduced sound, a natural sound, and an electronic sound.

VIDEO WITH PAPER PROTOTYPES

Our brains can be easily overwhelmed by visuals such as colors and brands. This is one of the reasons why paper prototypes can be successful. Removing complexity can help focus stakeholders on interaction and sound. With lo-fi video, a pen, paper, and video-editing software, it is easy to create understandable prototypes that convey abstract ideas with elements you can't see (sound) in a way (drawings) that won't distract or overwhelm the client with the look of branded elements (see Figure 9-3).

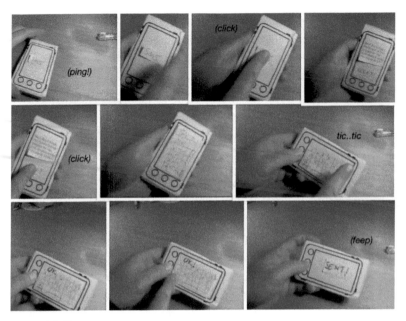

FIGURE 9-3

Paper prototypes reinforce the idea of an unfinished product with an unfinished sound palette. This paper prototype uses hand-drawn wireframes instead of a fully rendered interface. Sound effects are added to the video at the appropriate points, so the client can experience what the interactions might feel like in the final product.

You can use deliberately lo-fi demos and prototypes to present sound design within a given interaction, without the distraction of visual design and branding that might be incomplete, unknown, or incorrect. Asking stakeholders to close their eyes while listening to sounds is another way to ensure they're focusing entirely on the sounds and are not distracted by the visual elements.

Paper prototypes can also show how localized sounds can be used to represent an interaction between a user and a wall-sized touchscreen. A touchscreen is a very expensive piece of equipment, but it is possible to prototype the sound and interaction cheaply using a video with a paper prototype and sound overlay, as shown in Figure 9-4. In this example, an alert draws the user over, and she unlocks the interface with a gesture to see a list of images sent by a family member. She views them, selects one to keep, and then closes the interface.

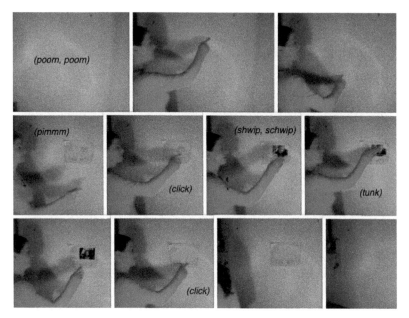

(poom, poom)

(pimmm)

(shwip, schwip)

(click)

(tunk)

(click)

FIGURE 9-4

Video stills from a person testing a paper prototype of a wall-sized product interface. The video has different interaction sounds edited in to sync the interactions with the sounds.

ANIMATION

Animation can work well as a level up in sophistication from paper prototyping, or if stakeholders or user testers don't react well to paper prototypes. Similar to paper prototyping, animation can simplify some of the visual aspects so that the stakeholders and user testers don't concentrate on them. Consider animating the product and user interaction and including the different suggested sounds.

In the last few decades, technology has given us ways to make animations quickly and inexpensively. Animations can be delivered as a series of standalone files for stakeholders and user testers to compare, or they can be created as clickable, web-based prototypes including the suggested sounds and then integrated into user testing or stakeholder interviews.

BINAURAL RECORDING

Binaural recording allows you to re-create from a first-person perspective what it feels like to be in a given environment, whether that is a car, subway, or ocean. It uses special microphones that are placed on—or right outside—your ears, or on the ears of a special dummy head. The microphones record left and right channels, capturing sound in a similar way to how we hear it. When the sound is played back over headphones, we actually feel like we are experiencing it firsthand.

Binaural recordings can help with the prototyping process by adding context to playback. You can record the experience of hearing the sound in a vehicle, for instance, and then play it back to your stakeholders in the conference room for a "3D stereo sound sensation."

One way to create an immersive sound testing experience is to use binaural microphones to record a sequence of interactions, for instance, with a vehicle—including opening the car door, starting the engine, and then interacting with the touchscreen—playing the sound effects in the vehicle to see how they are affected by its shape and materials.

The resulting demo could include a binaural recording of someone approaching a car, opening the door, getting in, and starting the engine:

1. *Crunch, crunch, crunch.* Feet approach the car on gravel.

2. *Clack-dunk.* The door opens.

3. *FUMP!* The door closes and is followed by the jangle of keys, *click-CHMM.*

4. *Vrooom!* The motor starts, and then the demo sounds begin to play.

REAL-WORLD PROTOTYPES

Sometimes, even realistic reproductions of the audio environment of a sound are not enough. Playing the sounds in the real world where they will be installed is the closest thing to experiencing the full product in an actual interaction (Figure 9-5).

FIGURE 9-5

Developing an in-car startup sound for a Chinese card brand

Hearing the sound in its intended context can help people make a clear decision then and there, saving enormous amounts of time and improving buy-in later on. There is nothing like this kind of hands-on, in-person review to streamline the decision-making process.

For example, during one in-car audio design exercise, the prototype sounds eventually made their way to the top level of stakeholders who would make the final decision on which design to use. As the executives sat, all wearing suits, in a brand new car with its unique new car smell, the three audio choices were played with the three final design options, narrowed down through the design process. One of the executives asked a few questions, consulted with his colleagues, and said, "Play the second one again. Okay, yeah, that's it. That is the one we ship," and then they all piled out of the car. The whole process took less than 10 minutes.

Because this particular sound design project was so complex, it went through most forms of prototypes listed in this chapter. First, it made use of prerecorded sounds in an interactive palette. Second, it used video with a sound overlay. Third, it used a binaural recording of the inside of the vehicle to bring the stakeholders further into the context. Fourth, the stakeholders made their final decision in the context of a real-world prototype.

Conclusion

Audio prototyping is an affordable, flexible, and fast way to demo different kinds of audio interactions for stakeholders and users. It is crucial for design, helpful for user testing, and useful for determining whether specific sounds might cause complications with hardware specifications. Prototyping makes it possible to easily swap out sounds for others before a product is finalized, and should be easy to come back to as needed during the sound design process. We'll focus on hardware and user testing in the next two chapters, and you'll want to bring along your prototypes there.

Hardware Testing

A CRUCIAL STEP OF the sound design process is hardware testing. This chapter should give you a good understanding of how the hardware will function, and serve as a guide on how to diagnose and fix a number of common problems related to distortion, playback hardware, and client expectations.

The testing phase consists of quality control, synchronization, and tuning. Testing helps identify not just the performance but the character of the audio hardware you're designing for.

When you don't have access to quality speakers, it is important to work within your hardware limitations. Limit instrumental tone color to what sounds good on the target hardware. Work with frequencies that don't cause the internal components of the speakers to rattle when played. Avoid sudden onset transients like the clang of a bell, the thump of a snare, or the heavy hammer of a piano note.

How Speakers Work

A typical speaker consists of a permanent magnet, an electromagnet, a frame, and a cone (see Figure 10-1). The responsive component of the speaker, which converts signals into sound, is a copper coil wrapped around Kapton, a fire-resistant polymer material that replaced the paper used in pre-1970s speakers, making them less likely to catch fire. This component is the electromagnet of the speaker, also called a *voice coil*. The voice coil is attached with flexibility of movement to the frame, attached rigidly to the speaker cone, and suspended above the permanent magnet at the base of the speaker.

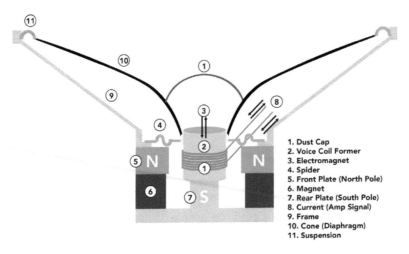

1. Dust Cap
2. Voice Coil Former
3. Electromagnet
4. Spider
5. Front Plate (North Pole)
6. Magnet
7. Rear Plate (South Pole)
8. Current (Amp Signal)
9. Frame
10. Cone (Diaphragm)
11. Suspension

FIGURE 10-1

How a speaker works. It's possible to overwhelm a cheap speaker with a loud sound (such as the onset transient of a piano note), causing distortion.

The electrical current running to the voice coil is an alternating current, which causes the poles to rapidly reverse position. This makes the magnets attract and repel each other, causing the voice coil to move back and forth, rapidly vibrating the cone and creating sound waves.

Quality Speakers

There are many differences between cheap and expensive speakers. Quality speakers:

- Do a great job of reproducing accurate instrumental tone color.

- Have a large dynamic range and can faithfully reproduce the wide range of sound the human ear can experience. Top-quality speakers use different-sized cones for high, medium, and low frequencies.

- Are able to reproduce a large set of frequencies without distortion. You might find that turning up the volume of a low-quality speaker causes sound to distort. That is because the signal overwhelms the speaker's capability. Low frequencies take more energy to produce than high frequencies, so cheap speakers and hardware alarms often operate in the higher end of the spectrum. It is more expensive to create a speaker that can reproduce the deep thundering noise of low bass frequencies.

- Can convey a sense of the acoustic space in which the recording was originally made. You can hear the reverb, room size, and position of instruments in the room.

- Include vibration insulation. Some of the cost of a quality speaker can be attributed to the materials, such as wood and metal, from which its cabinet is built, as well as attention given to the construction, fit, shape, and insulation of the cabinet walls. The speaker diaphragm creates intense vibrations in order to produce sound waves, so the cabinet must be constructed so as to not add any vibrations of its own.

Low-Quality Speakers

A lot of people record and play back sounds on their laptop speakers, which miss a lot of the low end (see Figure 10-2).

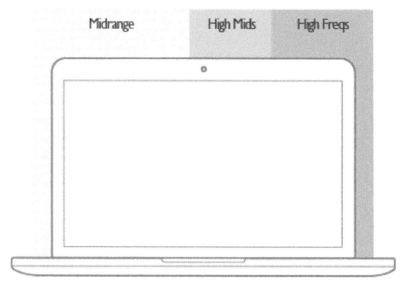

FIGURE 10-2

The range of typical laptop speakers is mostly mid to high frequencies. Testing sound with a laptop setup can miss bass frequencies.

Laptop speakers are not powerful enough to produce low frequencies at high enough decibels to create a full sound in playout. It's a good idea to have at least one "studio monitor" to test on while designing sounds.

Studio monitors are quality speakers that allow you to hear sounds in high definition, and they are used in studios for mixing, mastering, and sound creation (see Figure 10-3).

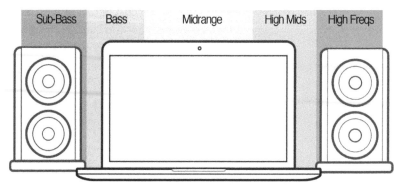

FIGURE 10-3
Studio monitor speakers can give you a better understanding of sound than laptop speakers, because they produce a fuller range of sound without distortion.

If you are designing sounds with low frequencies and only have a laptop for demonstrating them, then using headphones will allow you to hear those frequencies better than the laptop speakers alone. In this case, a good pair of noise-cancelling headphones will allow you to hear sounds in an uninterrupted environment, and can be helpful to focus clients' attention when you're playing back sounds in echoey conference rooms with lots of background noise.

Sound Channels and Playback Types

Each different type of sound and target hardware requires a different process. Let's look at each speaker configuration in a little more detail:

Mono

Mono simply means that the sound is coming out of a single channel. This is usually the case for products like microwaves, ovens, or alarm clocks where the sound comes out of one speaker.

Stereo

Stereo means that sound is coming out of two speakers, and you can mix different sounds for different speakers and hear them in the left or right channel. This simple setup can provide a sense of movement and space as different sounds pan back and forth from one channel to another.

Surround sound

Surround sound literally surrounds the listener. For a spatial sound system in a museum, for example, a quadrophonic (or 4.0 surround sound) approach will result in high-quality, immersive sound that can be mixed to four independent channels. The system consists of four speakers, one in each corner of the room (see Figure 10-4).

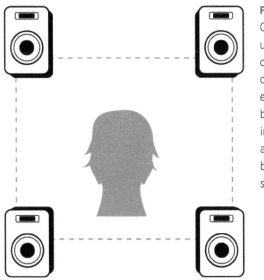

FIGURE 10-4
Quadraphonic sound uses four unique channels of audio to create an immersive experience. It can be used in museum installations, airports, and art exhibits to bring people fully into sound.

More sophisticated surround sound systems are commonly used for film and home theaters because they can play back dialogue and sound effects in separate channels. A 5.1 surround sound system includes six speakers, while 7.1 surround sound system adds two more speakers for a total of eight. These systems may also be used in auditoriums.

Binaural sound

Binaural recordings, covered in Chapter 9, are recorded through special microphones that you can wear on your ears just as you would headphones. You can also place these microphones on a dummy head to record sound. Binaural recordings are useful for playing back sounds as they'll be experienced in person. Want to hear what a microwave sounds like when you're in front of it? How about in another room? Playing binaural recordings is a useful way to help clients understand the experience of hearing a product's sound.

As a rule of thumb, test the sounds on the playout setup that will be used in the final product. If you know that you are designing for mono playback, not stereo, it is recommended that you make design decisions while listening on a single studio-quality speaker. All other things being equal, playing sounds on a single speaker eliminates problems, such as phase coherence, that can be created by playing sounds on two speakers.

Two speakers will give you stereo, which is important for designing sounds that use left and right channels of audio. Surround sound adds multiple speakers placed around the room, whereas quadraphonic sound uses four unique channels of audio to create an immersive experience.

If you are creating a sound for multiple sound setups—some of them stereo, some of them mono—make sure to check the mix for the mono. Converting a stereo sound to mono can introduce *phase cancellation* of your lower frequencies, making it sound uncharacteristically thin, which makes it have less of an impact. Although eliminating this problem is beyond the scope of this book, check with a sound designer if you think this might be an issue. They can work with the original sound file to convert it from stereo to mono more successfully.

Headphones allow you to listen to mono, stereo, or binaural sounds, depending on how the sound was recorded.

Testing the Target Hardware

You can save a lot of time and money by testing your designs as early as possible on the target hardware. This will calibrate all stakeholders' expectations to the same level.

Do not choose sounds that will constitute your product's auditory experience only by listening to them through a nice stereo system or through the speakers of a laptop. Nuances that might be clear while you're auditioning sound on high-quality hardware might not be apparent at all on the target hardware. Instead, make a point of listening to your sounds over the actual hardware in a variety of contexts. Otherwise, there may be a disconnect between expectations and actual playout.

If you don't already have a contact in engineering, ask for one. If the hardware is settled, consider using it for demonstrations and making your design decisions. If the hardware isn't settled, consider holding off on designing sounds until you have a good idea of the frequency landscape you're working with.

Design your sound set with the expectation that audio hardware will be improving in the future. In practice, this means creating a range of sounds, with some elements that are too rich, complex, or "ambitious" for current limitations. This will allow you to ensure that there is something ready to take advantage of future improvements in hardware. It also allows decision makers to experience what a product could achieve in later releases with small additional investments in hardware.

Testing for Distortion

Every sound is distorted to some degree.

Unless you are in an acoustically perfect space (which does not exist) with nothing occupying it except for the source, any sound that is produced is modified by the time you hear it. For the most part, this is not a problem—our brains are good at filtering out modest amounts of distortion and spotting the content, or "signal," contained within. This allowed our ancestors to identify the rustle of potential prey against the backdrop of wind blowing through the trees. Today it lets us pick out the song on a static-filled radio station, or concentrate on a conversation in a noisy restaurant. We are good at this kind of filtering, but it demands concentration and effort.

With the advent of electronic amplification, potential sources of distortion have multiplied. Distortion can take many forms: echoes, static, compression artifacts (like the "robotic" sound of a voice over Skype), or poor equalization that alters the tone quality. When sound is too bright, rumbly, or tinny, your brain must compensate to understand what it's "supposed" to sound like. This is why playing music in a car with the treble or bass all the way up feels vaguely unsettling.

In each case, the more noise there is, the more mental effort we must put into filtering out the signal. This is where thoughtful sound design can have a real, profound impact on our lives, beyond simply making things "sound nicer."

WHAT CAUSES DISTORTION?

Distortion is when the speaker cannot play back the sound in the way it was produced. The audio waves distort in some way and do not sound the way they were intended by the sound designer. You've heard this before with low-quality speakers when you turn the volume all the way up. Transients are one of the leading causes of distortion. We introduced transients in Chapter 8, but we'll go into further detail here.

DISTORTION AND TRANSIENTS

Things like snare drums and piano notes might cause a low-quality playout system to exhibit transient distortion. You might say that the amplifier is "too slow" to handle the onset or the start of a sound, if the initial buildup is very fast.

In other words, high-intensity onset transients such as those caused by piano notes may overwhelm speaker hardware, causing distortion; see Figures 10-5 and 10-6.

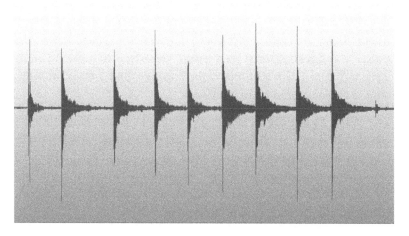

FIGURE 10-5

These are piano notes played slowly, with separation between them. You can see the onset transient that happens when the hammer hits the string of the piano, and the overtones from vibration of the string as it loses energy.

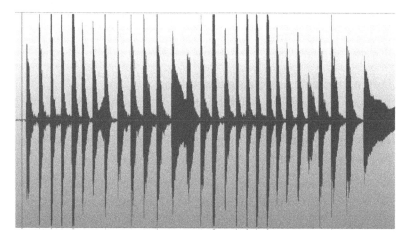

FIGURE 10-6

Piano notes are examples of fast, powerful transients. Playing piano notes very quickly together can result in distortion that overwhelms microphones and playback devices.

Hardware that has "good transient response" is just that: it is able to reproduce sharp transients in music, speech, or other sounds without distorting them.

If you are designing for a system that has poor transient response, try to use sounds that have a gentle onset rather than a sharp, fast start. Alternatively, you can use dynamic compression to "push down" that transient and prevent, or at least reduce, the effects of this kind of distortion. You can also turn down the attack or find a *transient shaper* plug-in for your audio-editing software.

Even when it's less drastic, the loss of transient information still has a significant impact on the perceived quality of a sound, and is a particular problem with audio such as MP3. At lower bit rates and/or with poor-quality encoding algorithms, transients in encoded audio suffer noticeably. Using compressors and limiters to "tame" sounds with strong transients is a common application.

A product's audio hardware quality has a direct effect on sound playout. The sum of all the audio hardware components is what determines the overall performance of the sound. Subpar elements like tiny speakers, underpowered amplifiers, and extremely band-limited frequency response have been the hobgoblins of sound designers for a long time—especially on mobile devices—but as mentioned earlier, this area is rapidly evolving. As we'll discuss next, there are now ways to mitigate the negative effects of distortion and poor transient response.

Soften transients or increase onset times

If your target hardware is going to have tiny speakers (which is often the case), avoid sounds that rely on lots of energy in the bass frequencies to deliver your message, or change the design to feature sounds with longer onset times.

Low-quality audio hardware can also impact transient response—the ability to change volume very rapidly—so loud sounds that reach their full volume quickly might end up distorting. The basic limitations of physics mean that lower frequencies need larger drivers. Don't rely on a lot of high-frequency information if you know that the playout hardware won't reproduce it faithfully.

Use hardware onboard processing to modify sounds

If there is *digital signal processing* (DSP) available on the target hardware, it will likely have some basic equalization controls, which have probably been configured with presets. Investigate these presets and listen to how they sound when turned off or changed. Small tweaks to basic equalization and volume performance on the playout hardware might take your sound from "meh" to "okay!"

If your sounds are going to play on different kinds of target hardware, you'll need to compare how the audio sounds on each piece of hardware. One way to test these differences is to play white noise through the speaker of each device, and then record the output (Figure 10-7).

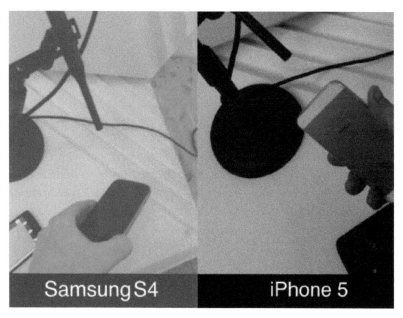

FIGURE 10-7
White noise played through the speakers of two different phones, then recorded through an external mic.

Analyze each device's audio performance. You're looking for peaks, or how much it distorts the white noise. The less it distorts the white noise, the better (Figure 10-8).

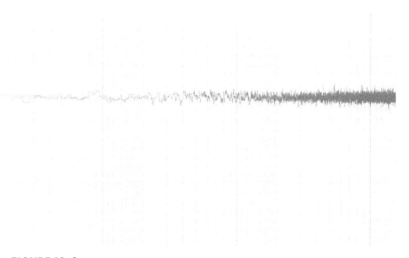

FIGURE 10-8
This is the ideal response for white noise through speaker hardware.

In Figure 10-9, you can see significant differences between the play-back hardware on the Samsung S4 compared to the iPhone 5. This illustrates the often stark difference between playback hardware on similar devices.

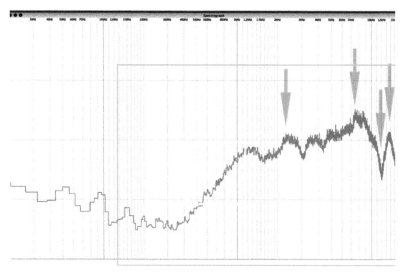

Samsung S4

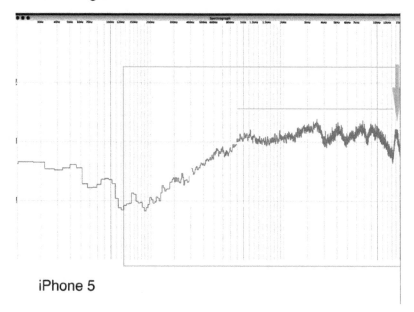

iPhone 5

FIGURE 10-9

These images show how much better the quality of the iPhone's hardware
speaker response is. You can see the peaks of the audio versus the room noise
on the left.

You'll want to equalize your sounds for each playback device and model to remove distortion and to ensure consistency across sound sets on multiple devices (Figure 10-10).

FIGURE 10-10
Applying corrective equalization levels out the speaker response by applying a curve opposite to the peaks.

You can modify the sound through an equalizer in the software you used to create the sound, before loading it onto the hardware. Or, depending on what DSP capabilities are built into the playback hardware, you can modify it there.

Design with distortion

If you can't change the target hardware and you're working within limited constraints, you will have to design *with* distortion. Here's one example of where coauthor Aaron Day made distortion work.

In 2007 Day designed what became a de facto signature for the Sprint-Samsung Instinct smartphone, one of the first touchscreen phones to follow the iPhone. The ringtone entered popular culture and eventually took on a life of its own.

Along with a fresh visual and physical design, stakeholders wanted some new, iconic ringtones—something that "really jumped from the phone." Unfortunately, the sound quality of the device wasn't capable of playing sharp transients loudly without noticeable distortion.

The product needed a solution that had a lot of energy but didn't rely on loud, sharp transients, and that sounded good even when distorted. The phone was intended for use in cars and in public, so it needed to cut through a purse or jacket pocket, and be able to overcome background noise.

After a few experiments with different basic waveforms, Day realized that a big fat synthetic sawtooth wave would be the best foundation. Sawtooth waves contain even and odd harmonics, which makes them sound "full." While the ringtone featured some electronic drum sounds, it was the sawtooth bass line that gave it energy.

Day also borrowed a technique from dance music that he calls the "octave bounce," a bass line that jumps up and down an octave every eighth note, creating a progression that sounds something like *rooo DEE rooo DEE rooo DEE* and is frequently used in disco remixes and as background music in high-energy advertising.

This combination of approaches worked well within the constraints: sawtooth waves sounded good when distorted or with their high frequencies attenuated, and the octave bounce had such a strong rhythmic and melodic identity that it was recognizable even when muffled. Day also tuned the fundamental note of the bass line so that it sounded as good as possible within the cavity resonance of the phone. The result was a ringtone that sounded fresh and full even when distorted.

Users liked it, and after a while the ringtone became popularly associated with the phone. It became the signature to let you know "an Instinct is ringing," much like the marimba ringer on the early iPhone. Not only did users of the Instinct record internet videos of themselves dancing to the ringtone but at least one person sampled the ringtone, looped it, and overdubbed lyrics about...ringtones!

Use the Missing Fundamental

As we discussed in Chapter 3, one way to improve the sound of low-quality speakers is to use a psychoacoustic technique to create the perception of a bass note that is not actually there. When we hear the third and fifth harmonic of a chord, our brain automatically fills in the missing information, giving us a rich perception of the fundamental note. Because this does not rely on the speaker hardware at all, it always sounds excellent, regardless of where it is played. To remind yourself of how this sounds, listen to "Rubber Soul" for that characteristic "Beatles bass."

Final Tuning

Often, by the time sound in a product is considered, the hardware requirements have already been set; or even worse, they're still in flux and completely out of your remit. If this is the case, be prepared to break some principles.

This section lists things you can do to improve the perceived audio quality of your product, organized by relative difficulty. These tips work for most situations where you need to tune the audio user interface of a consumer-facing device or digital product.

TEST OR MODIFY THE SOUND SOURCE

You can change the quality of what is played by modifying your sound file or the code that generates the sound. Depending on your specific project, this could easily be ranked after the second or even third suggestion, but it's listed first because problems that you only need one person to solve generally get fixed quicker and easier than if you need more people.

CHANGE THE INTERACTION LOGIC

You can change when, why, and if sound is played. For example: instead of making an alert louder and playing it only once, enable it to play at a lower volume three times in a row. This is a useful way to make the most of existing sounds and to modify them to create a user interface that works well.

TEST THE PLAYOUT SOFTWARE AND WORK WITH DSP

The digital part of your product's playout capability, which might contain built-in DSP, can offer parameterized control of audio processing that could benefit your sound.

For example, say you have delivered a sound to be used in a mobile device and the client complains that there isn't enough bass. You know that the small speaker has no way of moving enough air to make users feel low frequencies. However, you also know that there is likely a software-controlled high-pass filter somewhere before the sound reaches the speaker. A 12 dB/oct high-pass filter with a cutoff frequency of 900–1,100 Hz is typical in many small or mobile devices that have an audio user interface. This doesn't leave much, if any, room for what someone would call "warmth." Many of these filters have been set too conservatively. Sometimes, dropping the cutoff frequency only a few hundred hertz can make the sound be perceived as fuller.

This kind of tuning is program-dependent. Since audio hardware is more likely to distort when operated near its limits, material that has very fast transients or other dynamic changes may not work with lower cutoff frequencies. This approach takes advantage of the difference between what the hardware can produce and what it is specified to do in the software. Don't expect a tiny speaker to start producing bass just because you dropped the high-pass filter—it's still a tiny speaker but this should help.

Finally, if you lower the cutoff frequency of a high-pass filter to fix one problem, make sure that it doesn't introduce another, like speaker damage. For instance, some hardware-based audio filters are there for a reason—to protect the speakers from damage from high-energy transients and other sounds that might overwhelm the hardware.

SET LIMITS ON VOLUME

If you set a hard limit on maximum volume, you'll be able to control distortion and potential damage to device hardware.

TEST OR IMPROVE THE HARDWARE

Hardware improvement is one of the most obvious solutions, but also one of the most difficult to implement. At scale, even small changes can significantly affect costs. Any changes at this level of a project will almost always trigger budget and quality assurance alarms. Even if you discover a way to make a change that improves audio quality and lowers costs, changes in hardware design can require the retesting or recertification of engineering that was already considered "done."

It's not just about sound quality: better hardware increases the range of frequencies to sonify information. With a greater frequency range, you can still meet compliance but also increase the range of "words" the alerts can output.

Improving hardware is not just about speaker quality, either: it can be in the form of subtractive design, such as adding noise-insulating materials or improving component fit. It can also take the form of a passive component, such as weights that help give car doors that satisfying "thunk."

These changes may dramatically improve the product but are likely to increase the cost. If you are on the design side of the problem, you should probably accept that, unless you find a "showstopper" of a reason that justifies the additional expense, you aren't going to get the hardware changed. More often, you'll need to find creative solutions, such as making sure your design works as well as possible within the performance constraints of the product.

CHANGE OR MODIFY THE HARDWARE CONTAINER

You'll face the same problems changing or modifying the hardware container as with the playout hardware just discussed—except now the product manager, industrial designer, and possibly brand departments may need to approve any changes.

If you do change or modify the hardware container, you'll have to retune your sounds through the cavity resonance process.

ENSURE SOUNDS ARE ASSOCIATED WITH INTERACTIONS

Go through all states of the product and ensure that all audio and haptics mapped to interactions play out correctly.

PERFORM STRESS TESTING

Press the buttons really quickly to simulate a child playing with a device, or someone using the device in frustration, and see how the hardware and playback software handle the interactions.

TEST MULTIPLE SOUNDS AT ONCE

Can the playback hardware play sounds on top of each other, or only one sound at a time? If your product allows multiple sounds to play simultaneously, consider how they sound together, or whether one sound might need to stop before another one starts.

TEST SYNCHRONIZATION

When you're playing a video game, you're often in a state of flow. Imagine playing *Super Mario Brothers* and jumping into the air for a coin. If the coin collection sound doesn't happen, you'll be shaken out of the game world, and it can affect your gameplay. A delayed sound is even worse, and can diminish your experience of the game. Instead of jumping at the appropriate time, you might end up jumping late, missing the coin, or landing on an enemy. The same thing can happen when haptic signals are not lined up properly with the sound or the visual event. In each of these cases, the mismatch can be more than just irritating—it can be infuriating, ruining the entire experience by obscuring it with a difficult cognitive task: trying to match two events that should be concurrent but are not.

To ensure ideal user interactions on a mobile device, you'll want to measure synchronization between vibration and sound (see Figure 10-11). Fortunately, there's an easy way to do this.

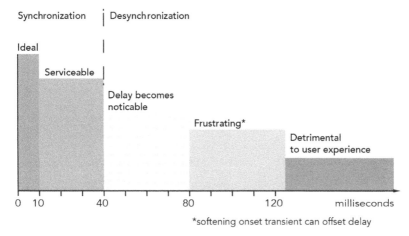

FIGURE 10-11
Ideal synchronization times for interactions.

First, you will need two microphones. Use rubber bands or something similar to attach a microphone to the device. If the device uses haptics and you know where to find the haptic motor, place the microphone capsule close to that. Set the device with its rubber-banded mic on some thick foam or stacked cloth, with the speaker facing up. Use a stand to position the second microphone over the device's speaker.

Now, perform whatever interactions you want to test for. You will see clearly on your audio-editing software's waveform display the points at which you physically interact with the device. For example, if it has a touchscreen, you will see screen touches as a "bump" in the waveform display for the first microphone. This will be followed by a haptic pulse and sound. It is the time difference between the touch event, the haptic response, and the sound that determines how well the three modalities fuse (see Figure 10-12).

[TIP]

These examples assume that you want sound and vibration to fuse, and are able to make them do so.

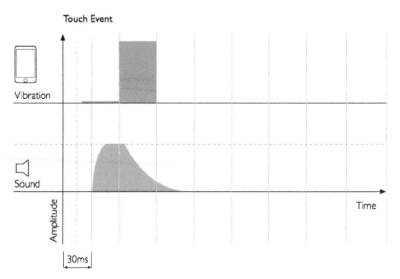

FIGURE 10-12

Synchronizing a sound and vibration to a single touch event. In this case, the sound and haptic feedback should fuse, in order to create a subtle but vital enhancement of the keypress experience.

A light switch is an easy way to think about the many types of information a person experiences when they interact with even a simple device. You click a light switch and the mechanical sound matches your action. You feel a snap, hear a click, and see a light come on. These things don't actually all happen at the same time. At the microsecond level, the gaps between the events are significant. However, since they are within a millisecond or two of each other, we experience perceptual fusion and call them "one."

In the cases where perceptual fusion isn't possible or would feel sloppy if implemented, it is best to decorrelate entirely and make the parts distinct. With these longer intervals, where the sound and haptic element are separated enough in time that at least one transient from each is distinct, you can think of them as two parts of a whole.

Many things in our lives that we interact with display these kinds of micro-rhythmic characteristics. Latches, door locks (*ka-schack!*), punch buttons, and many plastic closures are excellent examples.

[TIP]

Don't forget to test for delays while the device is running other programs.

It is always possible for extra computational load to affect synchronization of haptics and sound. Always test the synchronization of the product while it is experiencing high demand on the processor.

Retest everything after you've made any changes, using the flowchart in Figure 10-13.

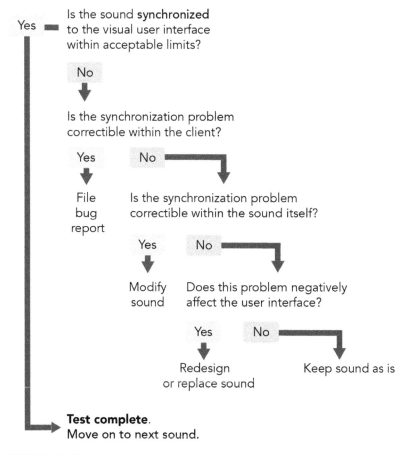

FIGURE 10-13
Synchronization flowchart for checking each sound.

Conclusion

Testing hardware might be a tedious process, but it is just as crucial as testing the user experience (which you'll learn about in the next chapter). All sounds are limited by the frequency range of playout hardware, the speaker response profile, and the product's casing or cabinet. Applying the concepts in this chapter will allow you to work with limited hardware, distortion, and the product's shape in order to make products that sound consistently good.

[11]

User Testing

When we launched the first Jambox at Jawbone, we thought we were so smart in proactively telling people when the battery was low. That was all good, but when real people started using it, they didn't turn it off at night and so we'd get reports of this booming, scary voice at 3 a.m., which some people thought was an intruder. Test your product. Test with real people. Test in real settings and contexts.

—KAREN KAUSHANSKY, JAWBONE

User testing is important.

It is helpful to inform your design by looking at actual user behavior instead of solely gathering decontextualized feedback. Proponents of the Lean Startup method, for example, are skeptical of the utility of asking people to predict their own behavior, and prefers to give people real options and see what they actually do. Some market research and survey responses can be unavoidable in development, but keep in mind that nothing quite replaces observation of real-world use.

The user testing process for sound design is a way to iteratively test soundscapes and design choices at various product stages. It's faster and less expensive to test sounds before they're put into the finished device to make sure the sound fits the interaction. Stakeholder listening sessions, web feedback sessions and small focus groups allow for initial decisions to be validated or tossed out. Giving stakeholders a condensed summary of feedback can help provide an external perspective and inform design direction from beyond the conference room. Once user feedback is collected, the most successful soundscapes can be integrated into prototypes that can be tested in context. The last stage of the user testing process is when the product is ready for production and the final sounds and interactions are tested. This stage, along with hardware testing (discussed in the previous chapter), completes the sound design process.

Researching the Domain

If you're developing sounds for an unfamiliar product or experience, it is crucial to develop an understanding of the different uses and history of your product as well as the general sentiment for what's currently available on the market.

Take whatever you know already, and gather viewpoints from varying perspectives and backgrounds. It's important to recognize that you have an individualized bias no matter where you come from. Understand if there is an existing hypothesis about what makes for a good product in your category, and acknowledge that there might be more than one solution to the problem you are trying to solve.

Testing for Inclusivity

Considering universal design and addressing the needs of many versus the needs of the few promotes the development of widely used products that both make money and improve people's lives.

Aiming for inclusivity genuinely does improve the world for everyone. For example, wheelchair ramps are equally useful for people with push-carts, those pushing strollers, or those who use wheelchairs. Automatic doors are equally useful for the elderly and a new parent carrying a child in one arm and a bag of groceries in the other.

Universal design accounts for those of different abilities. Note that there may be not only permanent disabilities, but also situational disabilities (like the case of the new parent) or temporary limitations (such as a broken limb) that hinder a person's capacity to perform certain functions for a limited period of time (see Figures 11-1 and 11-2):

Permanent limitations

Permanent limitations are those where the loss of ability is unrecoverable. When someone is born without or loses the use of a limb, sight, or hearing, these are fixed, unchangeable situations.

Temporary limitations

Some people experience hearing loss in one or both ears as they get older, or a very loud sound can cause hearing loss for a short period of time. These can be temporary limitations, and in these cases, products need to rely on different senses to get information across.

Situational limitations

As people move through different environments, their abilities can also change dramatically. A bartender might not be able to hear an order come across the counter because of ambient noise. A caller might not be able to hear a voice on the other end of the phone when a noisy truck drives by. These are situational limitations. We can design better sounds or better environments, and understand the role sound can play in addressing situational limitations.

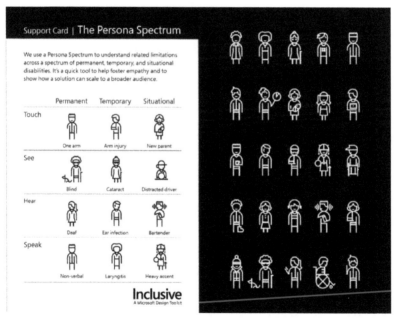

FIGURE 11-1

Examples of permanent, temporary, and situational signal blockages and possible causes (© Microsoft 2016, used with permission).

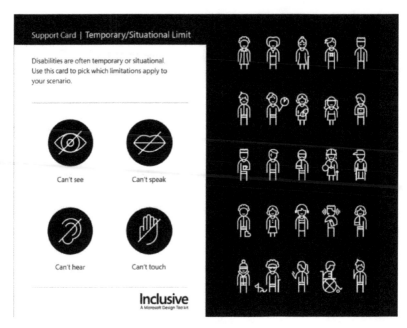

FIGURE 11-2

Activity card for temporary/situational limitations (© Microsoft 2016, used with permission).

When temporary limitations, situational challenges, and permanent disabilities are considered as a group including hearing loss, blindness, visual impairments, ADD, autism, mobility disabilities, and dyslexia, the number of people affected reaches 21 million in the US alone, and 1 billion worldwide.[1]

When the use of technology is tested among working age adults, the majority—79%—report experiencing some difficulty with technology. It is essential that your user testing is targeted to assess the ease of use of your product for those with limitations.

Contextual User Testing

We bring our technology with us into different contexts, family situations, and times of day. We need technology that works well in optimum situations as well as edge cases. Because sound is so intensely

---

1 Anant Maheshwari, "AI for a billion people. And an accessible world," Microsoft, *http://bit.ly/2RBaHs4.*

specific to context, it is crucial to test in the real world, or as close to it as you can reasonably get. Contextual user testing deals with interactions that happen because of time of day, location, noise levels, accessibility issues, or seasonal differences. Each context can influence how a sound affects someone—specifically, whether the sound is intrusive, ignored, or welcomed (see Figure 11-3).

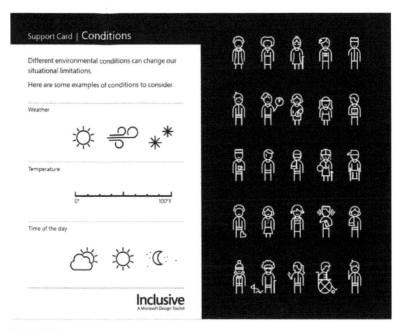

FIGURE 11-3
Microsoft activity card with considerations for different conditions
(© Microsoft 2016, used with permission).

Contextual testing works best when users can take the product home with them or use it on a daily basis. Unless you know the exact context and hardware for a given audio experience, design for ranges of context rather than ideals. Users often hear sounds in situations that are far from optimal, in terms of both environment and hardware: you may be testing in a quiet room over a pair of high-quality speakers, but your users might be listening over a smartphone loudspeaker in a noisy coffeehouse. Take your product out into the real world and test it. Test it with real people. Test it with friends of friends. Play with it on public transportation. Take it into an office, a (relatively quiet) bar, or a grocery store. The results may be surprising (see Figure 11-4).

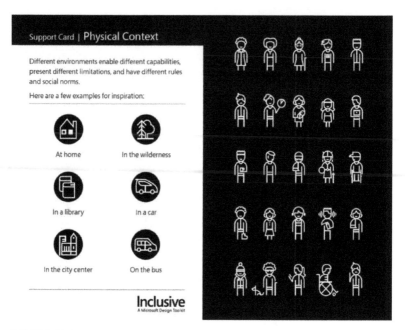

FIGURE 11-4

Inclusions for different locations. How will a technology work off-grid in the wilderness? (© Microsoft 2016, used with permission.)

Testing in a purse or backpack

If you're making a portable object that makes a sound, consider how placing it in a purse or backpack might alter the sound. Even a little bit of material or leather can dramatically reduce the high frequencies, making notifications more difficult to hear. One way to mitigate this is to add a haptic vibration to ensure that the notification will still be felt through the material.

Testing at various distances

In this test, you'll want to run through scenarios at various distances in order to understand how sounds work at close and far ranges, and how they might disturb people nearby. You might find out that the alarm clock you've designed carries very clearly through walls, annoying others in the apartment complex. Here are some possible scenarios:

- In-hand

- On a table

- Across the room

- In another room with the door open

- In another room, separated by a closed door made from cheap, hollow materials

- In another room, separated by a closed door made from solid materials

- In a large open space, like an office or train station

If you need something to be heard from another room and the product has the ability to either vibrate or create low frequencies, then bring these into your design.

Test sound designs close at hand, at medium distance, and through a wall or down the hallway (see Figure 11-5).

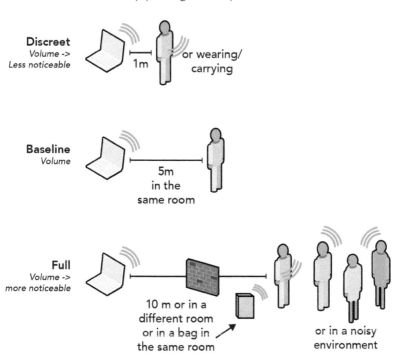

FIGURE 11-5

No matter what you're designing, you should test your product at different distances to see how it performs. Depending on how close you expect the user to be when the product makes a sound, you will want to adjust the volume of the device to be discreet, baseline, or full volume. Test your sound in a purse, backpack, or back pocket to see how it sounds. Test your sound in the same room as you to see how the sound performs close by and at a distance. Test your sound in a different room to see if you can (or cannot) hear it.

Products that vibrate can vibrate against surfaces they're resting on, making the vibration audible (think of a phone on a wooden table).

Testing on public transportation

This test is helpful for seeing how other people might hear your device in different public situations and how it might be bothersome. Go with a colleague and trigger a sound while you're sitting next to each other, across from each other, when the bus or train is full and noisy, and when it is empty and quiet.

Testing on a flight

If you have a member of your team traveling for work, have them test the sounds on the flight. Planes add a particular low hum to the environment that can disrupt certain sounds from coming through clearly. Given how ubiquitous this experience is, it can be worth testing specifically.

Testing in international environments and contexts

If you are planning to release a product to international markets, it is reasonable to expect that different populations will have different preferences and different associations for sounds. For instance, if you're developing a product that might be used in Seoul, you'll want to review cultural considerations of politeness and expectations of quietness (or electronic friendliness—for example, some Korean rice cookers play adorable tunes when finished). On the other hand, Korean service sounds do not work well in Europe and North America because they are perceived as too long and annoying in tone color and character.

[TIP]

One study on ringtones—"Soundscape Vision" from Samsung Electronics Corporation in 2006—found that "regardless of cultural differences and different user situation, certain attributes were regarded as important by respondents":

- Warm, subtle, deep tone colors and simple sounds
- Melodies that are progressive in loudness and structure
- Higher fidelity in playback

TEST FOR SOCIAL CONTEXT

Consider how the product might be used alone, with coworkers, in a crowd, or with friends and family (see Figure 11-6). The social norms when someone is alone are different than when someone's in a crowd, around close family or friends, and at the office. In the same way that people might adjust their behavior according to their environment, devices that go with us into these environments should be flexible to match our contextual interaction styles. A work alert for someone in a family context is a situational-technology mismatch.

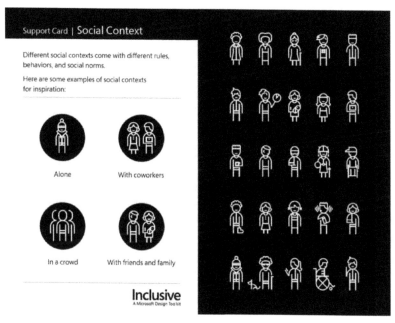

FIGURE 11-6

Inclusive design support card for designing with different social contexts. Consider how the product might be used alone, with coworkers, in a crowd, or with friends and family (© Microsoft 2016, used with permission).

Giving users the option to adjust or change the alert style or to turn off the alerts completely from a top-level menu can help them adjust seamlessly to social contexts alongside their devices. Here are some aspects to consider in different contexts:

Alone

Does the alert interrupt restful time? Does it distract from leisure activities?

With coworkers

> Does the sound of an incoming alert disrupt people nearby other than the intended recipient?

In a crowd

> Can the sound of the alert be heard above a crowd? Can it be heard in a loud environment? Would it potentially disrupt a wedding, funeral, or cultural event?

Friends and family

> Can the sound be turned off or changed? Does it intrude on personal time or romantic time?

At school

> Does the sound or notification interfere with classroom activities?

Devices are entities that we carry around with us, and they have their own behaviors. Training them to match our behaviors, and to respect changes in our needs or contexts, can help smooth their interactions with us. Creating a filter for messages is one way to organize attention into a range of channels, so that some are intrusive and high level, and others are not. As of 2018, typical smartphone alerts consist of the same *ping*, no matter the content, sender, or context. This means that there is no hierarchical difference between an urgent alert from the vet about a sick dog and an automated update from a gaming app about a new feature.

Allowing people to set priorities and alert styles according to who is sending the message—friends and family, work, or other businesses—is one way to conserve attention. Messages sent by friends should sound or feel different than work-based or automated alerts. These kinds of audio differences can give an initial indication about the message received. Similar to the Gmail folders that sort "Primary" from "Social" and "Promotions," diversification of alert styles can help users make better decisions about whether to check the alert based on the context.

Some applications have emoji and screen animations that appear, then grow, shake, and return to normal size. This is the emoji equivalent of making something "loud" and friendly. Another form of animation is message confetti, such as hearts or balloons that rise up from the bottom of the screen.

Haptics could take a cue from these friendly messages by providing options for combined events that include a kind of haptic animation, starting with a small tap and growing to a large swell, to signal that the message is friendly and human. These kinds of messages could be sent only by friends, with different forms used to signal joy, love, or an emergency.

Most users don't know this, but you can actually set custom vibrations on the iPhone. The Sounds and Haptics menu allows users to "record" a custom haptic style by tapping the phone. This allows users to set very nonintrusive text-message buzzes, making for a distinctive style of alert that is recognizable to the phone owner and also less invasive to others. It can also be made subtle enough that it is unnoticeable when the phone is in the user's pocket during other activities.

Segmentation and Applied Ethnography

Segmentation is a form of *ethnography*, or the study and description of the customs, tools, and rituals of people and groups across cultures. In *applied ethnography* you're trying to understand and catalog features that define that population. And if there are different opinions or different strategies that you observe within that population, it's useful to try to identify the relevant dimensions, or *segments*, that correlate with those differences.

Successful market research illuminates assumptions in the design of the product, or assumptions about its audience use cases that aren't accurate. Many researchers divide populations in irrelevant, stereotypical ways, such as by race, gender, or social class. Segmentation of this kind can easily overlook what people actually need. Instead, consider focusing on segmentation based on purpose or idea. Having a specific purpose indicates how to best craft a product for people because it's directed toward an end. These higher-level categories are more likely to span across cultures, backgrounds, and incomes, and the advantage of this approach is that it relates more to qualitative aspects of products.

Malcolm Gladwell's 2004 TED Talk "Choice, Happiness and Spaghetti Sauce"[2] highlights why both qualitative and quantitative research are necessary, and why the answer to a question might not be a single,

---

2 See *http://bit.ly/2Q07z8Q*.

perfect product, but a range of solutions. Good exploratory research will identify relevant segments with regard to the product or sound you are studying. Gladwell recounts the story of Howard Moskowitz, who was hired by the Campbell Soup Company to do market research for Prego back when all the food companies were trying to develop a single perfect pasta sauce (or single perfect mustard, etc.) for everyone. Moskowitz figured out that one segment of society preferred a *chunky* pasta sauce, while others preferred a *plain* pasta sauce. Yet another segment liked *spicy* sauce. The population divided roughly evenly, with about one-third preferring each category. At the time, no one was making a chunky pasta sauce, so the preferences of that segment of the population were going unmet. Once this was discovered, Campbell's could tailor its products more specifically to those groups. Instead of segmenting along race, gender, age, or income lines, Moskowitz worked to determine the preferences that ranged across traditional segmentations, creating a set of products that gave everyone a choice based on purpose and intention.

It is challenging to successfully identify segments within your demographics that give you more information than your original hypothesis, but it is a crucial way of discovering how to build products that meet people's needs.

Formats for User Testing

Testing potential sounds, soundscapes, and notifications before a product is built involves playing different sets of sounds to stakeholders or user testers in person or in a web survey format, gathering their feedback and recommendations, and condensing that information into excerpts and actionable steps. This can be done in different ways, either remotely or in person, using sounds alone or physical prototypes of the device.

ONLINE OR IN-PERSON SURVEYS

One of the great challenges of asking people to give feedback about creative efforts, such as graphic design or music, is that they generally want to be polite and not risk offense. Consider creating an online listening survey where your test group can "audition" the different brand-soundtracks, rate them from zero to four stars, and leave written feedback.

Whether you're testing in person or over the web, it's important to make sure your listeners experience the sounds in a similar context with similar playout technology (see Figure 11-7). This will avoid skewing the data with factors that can be prevented. For a web survey, you might tell people to set the volume to 40% of their device's max output, and to listen on Apple Airpods. Listening on a specific set of headphones negates many of the effects of context, such as room acoustics and environmental noise, while unifying the listening experience. The survey could also ask what headphones or earbuds users are listening on, and this information could be associated with reviews of the experience. Likewise, when testing in person, standardize the interface, playout, and listening hardware. For instance, you might give everyone a set of headphones and an iPad demo, and request that testers not change the volume during the demos.

Online Listening Survey

Thanks for participating in our listening survey!

During this survey, you'll hear four short tracks of music and you'll be asked for feedback about what you think of each track. There is no right or wrong response. We just want your honest opinion.

These responses are anonymous. We do not track any personal information of any kind.

Thanks again for your participation!

(Next)

FIGURE 11-7
Landing page and instructions for an online test tool used to play branded soundtracks for review. Requesting specific playout hardware ensures that the sounds are being heard the same by all participants. Alternatively, a survey could request details about the hardware that the user is playing the sounds on to be identified, in order to understand how specific hardware might alter the favorability of a given sound set.

Well-presented feedback is useful for convincing stakeholders to remove negatively reviewed sounds. Internal stakeholders might be attached to specific melodies or choices, and reviewers can give you the power to convince them to let go.

Remember that any presentation you deliver to a stakeholder will likely be shown again to someone else inside the company, without any accompanying description from you. Clear, simple presentations work better than complex ones that need elaborate explanation; see Figure 11-8 for a good example.

Dance Dynamic	Mysterioso	Passionata	Style
☆☆☆☆	☆☆☆☆	☆☆☆☆	☆☆☆☆
Listeners identified this as a fake U2 track immediately. While U2 is very popular, it does not resonate. This sound should be avoided.	The ambient elements of this track were appreciated. Rethink this track and explore more ambient sounds.	People described this track as "happy" but insincere. Explore the sparser aspects of the song.	Found this track too commercial and "Kenny G" sounding. Do not have any affinity for this sound. This sound should be avoided.

FIGURE 11-8
Presentation to client: summary of listener feedback from four different branded soundtracks. Reviewers were asked to rate the tracks from zero to four stars. The average of this was presented as an overall "grade" for each track.

ONE-ON-ONE SESSIONS

In-person user testing with prototypes works best one-on-one, with a designer present to observe and manage the test process. This method of testing is good for when the product is still being developed and you want to try alternatives or determine if your initial design hypothesis is heading in the right direction.

One-on-one user testing also works best with realistic questions. For instance, if you want to test the search function, say, "Your friend told you about Introduction to Photography 101, and you want to look it up," rather than, "Search for something that you find interesting." Have participants complete the exercises with as little involvement or direction from you as possible. Then, using the guidelines described in the next section, make observations about what it is they're doing.

Consider that small problems can cover up other problems

People might get stuck on initial problems and not even have an opportunity to get far in the user flow. People naturally gravitate toward the most prominent errors, those that are the most glaring and most central to the flows you're testing. Fix the initial challenges to see if they're covering up other issues.

Simulate busyness, stress, or distraction

People will often end up using a product when they are busy or stressed, but this can easily be missed during in-person testing. One way to simulate busyness is to give testers something difficult to do, like "Start with the number 17,000 and count backward by 13." To add stress, ask them to go faster. When your product is playing a sound or the user is trying to get something done, you'll be able to see very quickly whether the sound is annoying to them.

A word of caution here: although simulating stress might give you important feedback, your test subjects will not appreciate it, especially if you make them feel incompetent. Make sure you keep the well-being of your test subjects in mind as you design the stressor.

Determine user questions and executional components

If you're testing a new voice user interface product like Alexa, you have to assume that people don't know what to do with it. What voice commands are there? What are the product's limitations? How can you turn it off and on? In this case, you can try different terms for actions and test how recognizable the terms are.

How a stakeholder labels an interaction might be completely different from how a user sees it. When you're talking to users, they don't care about that. Users can learn how to say, "Hey Alexa" without ever knowing that, on the stakeholder side, "Alexa" is a *wake word*. All they need to know is how to get the device to pay attention to them. It's important to keep those labels clear among your stakeholders, though, and keep the terms aligned with how success is being measured for the project.

FOCUS GROUPS

Focus groups usually involve 8–10 people around a table or on couches being led through a discussion by a moderator. Sometimes the client will suggest focus groups, but they are often not as useful as one-on-one sessions. Remember that big personalities can sway opinion, whereas individual tests can make people more comfortable being honest about how they perceive your products. If you find that a single individual is dominating the conversation, consider not inviting them to future studies. Make sure to allow time for discussions with individual group members after the session. Consider spending more time with the quietest members of the group, as they may be the ones with the best listening skills, and produce solid perspectives and valuable ideas.

When using a group, 8–10 people is enough. Smaller groups are easier to track and communicate with, and they're easier to meet with more frequently. More than 10 or 12 people, and you'll see a lot of repeated observations. This doesn't mean that you won't learn anything new, but you will lose valuable development time and see diminishing results from the effort. It is more useful to iterate the product multiple times and gain new insights from small groups than perform fewer tests with large groups. Ensure that you have a diverse range of people in the group. Try to identify patterns and what drove certain decisions or actions. These are the areas to pay attention to.

When successful, open discussions can pave the way to new, unexpected results. If your stakeholders require focus groups, consider how general conversation might give people a vocabulary and shared experience with which they can make helpful assessments about the sounds devices make, or help direct a design focus for the overall project.

Research Your Personas

Personas are dangerous if you're just making them up. They need to be informed by market research and interviews. You need to have empathy for human lives and the difficulties people face, not just account for the times when things go right. Part of this process is finding useful markers. More and more there are properties that cross traditional boundaries—like with video games, where the defining feature is not related to age, gender, socioeconomic status, or ethnicity, but a new cultural mode of being.

There can be big differences between individuals assigned to the same demographic group. For instance, some millennials might still live with their parents, but many are well off and live alone. Some have children, or married early. To place everyone of a certain age group into the same persona ("millennial") misses the point. When developing products, functional definitions related to someone's values, context, and goals are more important than abstract categories. Make a product that works for a range of situations instead of one that works only on a demographic assumption. Then you'll have a product that can become a classic instead of a cloistered, brittle one.

REVIEW THE FINAL CHECKLIST

The best product testing involves sending a device home with testers so it can live with them for a while. Contextual testing is about simulating the environments and situations a technology may encounter during its lifetime. There are many issues to consider. Whether or not you perform a home test, review the following list to ensure you have covered everything in your studies.

Sound

- Poor sound quality (distorted)

- Wrong pitch (too high- or low-pitched, or a pitch that conflicts with the surrounding environment)

- Wrong volume (too loud or too quiet)

- Can the sound be turned off or changed?

Time

- Ill-timed (wrong place or situation, wrong time of day)

- Mismatched with the user interface (aesthetic or timing)

- Wrong duration (too long or too short)

- Played too frequently or too infrequently (Microsoft Outlook notification, stock ticker or energy usage, a dangerous truck backing up)

Attention

- Wrong level of urgency (too alarming/forcing attention or too subtle)

- Played without reason (does it inform?)

- Interruptive to others (a sound meant for a single person is played for many, sound travels through apartment walls, or sound goes off in a quiet theater)

- Is speech necessary to the success of the product? Does the addition of speech increase cognitive burden? Do you have the resources necessary for speech translation?

Inclusion

- Does the device still work for those with temporary, situational, or permanent disabilities? Those who can't see, speak, hear, or touch? Consider running the product test through Microsoft's Inclusive Toolkit activity cards.[3]

- Can the notification be changed to haptic, visual, or light-based depending on the needs of the user?

Conditions

- Does the device take into account time of day? Does it have sounds that will go off in the middle of the night? Does it take into context the sleep/wake cycle?

- How does the device perform in loud or quiet environments?

- Have you tested how the device sounds in another room, on public transportation, in the user's hand, or in a purse or backpack?

- Have you tested connected devices in areas with poor WiFi connectivity?

Presenting Your Findings to Stakeholders

One of the most important reasons for user testing is to get actionable content, but often this content can fill dozens of pages. You don't want to overwhelm your stakeholders, but you still want to be informative. Infographic presentations are useful for showing what you have learned clearly and concisely (Figure 11-9).

---

3 Microsoft Inclusive Design Toolkit, *http://bit.ly/2DqFRQ3*.

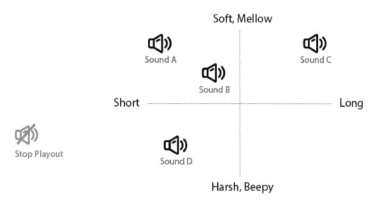

FIGURE 11-9

A client presentation. Focus group feedback was converted into a clickable interface so that the client could hear the sounds in context with the positioning assigned by the participants. Response summaries are organized in a different tab so that the client can see highlighted responses from participants.

Conclusion

User testing is an important way to test and reframe ideas or hypotheses you or your stakeholders have about a product. Preproduct testing is helpful when a range of solutions or scenarios has been developed and you need help deciding which one is best. With prototype testing, context is most important. Although one-on-one interviews are preferred, focus groups can have benefits as well. Be careful to consider how different sounds might need to be altered to fit different environments, ability levels, and cultural expectations.

User testing is also a valuable way to incorporate user feedback into the decision-making process. Don't overwhelm your decision makers with too much information, however. You'll want to give them direction and conclusions in a succinct, actionable way—such as with an infographic presentation—that helps move the product to production.

Recommended Reading

Jonathan Shariat and Cynthia Savard Saucier, *Tragic Design: The Impact of Bad Product Design and How to Fix It* (O'Reilly)

> As tech gets closer to every moment of our lives, the quality of interface design can determine life, death, or simply awkwardness. Great design can eliminate that. This book covers many ways companies get it wrong and what we can learn from them.

Cathy Pearl, *Designing Voice User Interfaces: Principles of Conversational Experiences* (O'Reilly)

> Designing voice interfaces involves a level of complexity and nuance that merits its own book.

Camille Moussette, *Simple Haptics: Sketching Perspectives for the Design of Haptic Interactions* (Umea Institute of Design)

> Mousette's text is one of the best books on prototyping nonvisual interactions. His insights about integrating haptics into user experience are thorough and inspiring.

Perry R. Cook, ed., *Music, Cognition, and Computerized Sound: An Introduction to Psychoacoustics* (MIT Press)

> This book provides an overview to get you on your way to understanding psychoacoustics. It is both accessible and deep. Highly recommended.

Andy Farnell, *Designing Sound* (MIT Press)

> If you want to learn about generative audio, this is a great place to start. Farnell explains the theory and practical aspects of using software to make generative and interactive sound.

F. Alton Everest, *Master Handbook of Acoustics* (McGraw Hill)

> This book goes into deep detail on all aspects of sound, including physics, perception, and creation. It is a complete resource for anything you'd like to learn about sound.

Reinier Plomp, *The Intelligent Ear: On the Nature of Sound and Perception* (Lawrence Erlbaum Associates)

An astonishing account of the new science of auditory perception that overturns old paradigms. An essential book for anyone who wants to understand the science of psychoacoustics.

[Index]

trademarks (sound). *See* sound and
brand
transients (component)
about, xxv, 107–110, 154–156
digital signal processing
and, 157–161
increasing onset times for, 156
softening, 156
as unwanted sounds, 65
transverse waves, 30
treacly (quality), xviii
treble (frequency range), xxvii, 19
tremolo, 58
triangle waves, 113–114
tubby (quality), xxii
tuning audio interface
about, 161
changing hardware container, 164
changing interaction logic, 162
ensuring sounds are associated
with interactions, 164
performing stress testing, 164
setting limits on volume, 163
testing/improving hardware, 163
testing/modifying sound
source, 162
testing multiple sounds at
once, 164
testing playout software, 162
testing synchronization, 164–167
working with DSP, 162
tuning forks, 106–107
The Tuning of the World (Scafer), 15
turbulence of air/fluid movement in
quiet products
airflow through products, 37–38
exhaust manifolds and, 36–37
exterior shape and, 35–36
laminar flow, 39–40
liquid flow through products, 38–
39
turgid (quality), xvii
turning off sound (silent mode), 177
20th Century Fox (company), 85–86

U

uBeam (company), 2
Ultra Nordic agency, 1–2
ultrasonic (frequency range), xxviii, 2
umami, 1
Universal Design, 114–124, 170

University of Colorado, 117
unused space in quiet products, 24
unwanted sound. *See* annoying
sound
upper bass (frequency range), xxvii
upper highs (frequency range), xxviii
upper middles (frequency range), xxvii
use cases, 128–129
user testing
about, 169–170
applied ethnography, 179–180
contextual, 172–180
designing for inclusivity, 170–
172, 186
preproduct, 180–182
presenting findings to stakeholders, 186–187
prototype, 182–184
researching personas, 184
researching the domain, 170
reviewing final checklist, 185–186
segmentation, 179–180

V

vague (quality), xxii
veiled (technical attribute), xxxiii
velvet fog (quality), xxii
vibration cancellation in quiet products, 29–34
vibrato, 57
violining (technical attribute), xxxiii
visceral (quality), xxi
Visual AI app, 124
visual-and-sound-to-haptic translation, 120
visual interface, 46, 129–130
visual-to-audio translation, 115–118
Vitamix (company), 28
vocal personality, 91–94
voice coil, 147–148
voice interfaces
recommended reading, 189
translating, 115–118
vocal personality in, 91–94
volume
reducing for alerts, 77–78
setting limits on, 163
vowel coloration, xxviii

[*About the Contributors*]

Karen Kaushansky is an experience designer and consultant working to define and design interactions—human–robot, speech recognition, conversational UIs, autonomous vehicles, and mixed reality—often 5 to 10 years before they are on most radars. She creates meaningful and connected experiences in the physical world, spanning hardware and software. She started designing voice and interactive audio experiences in 1996 and is currently consulting for multiple companies, pushing the boundaries in these areas. Past employers and clients include Tellme (Microsoft), Nuance, Jawbone, Samsung, Zoox, and LEGO. Kaushansky recently moved to Switzerland from San Francisco.

Walter Werzowa is an Austrian-born classically trained composer, conductor, and multi-instrumentalist based in Los Angeles. He penned the most recognizable sonic trademark in the world: Intel. Werzowa was one of six children, and the only one not trained as a doctor. He is catching up: after earning his master's degree in psychology, he built HealthTunes™, a streaming platform that delivers evidence-based clinical research with matching music to doctors and hospitals. He has also masterminded platinum records (Edelweiss) and collaborated on operas (Auszählreim).

Hannah Davis is a programmer, data scientist, and musician. She likes music generation, data visualization and sonification, natural language processing, machine learning, and storytelling in various formats. She is currently working on TransProse, a program that translates literature and emotional data into music, creating datasets for machine learning. Davis is also working on a project to generatively score films. Through her work on emotions in AI, she's become particularly interested in the idea of subjective data and has recently started further research into this area. She is a 2017 AI Grant recipient.

Jess Mitchell is senior manager of research and design, at the Inclusive Design Research Centre at OCAD University in Toronto. Her work focuses on fostering innovation within diverse communities while achieving outcomes that benefit everyone. She applies this inclusive and broad perspective along with extensive experience to managing large-scale international projects, focused organizational initiatives, and everything in between. With a background in ethics, Mitchell delivers a unique perspective on messy and complex contexts that helps organizations and individuals navigate a productive way forward.

Dan Crandall is an automotive technician who currently runs DCTech, a small auto repair shop. He is an ASE-certified Master Technician with 15 years of experience in the automotive repair, fabrication, and performance industries. He has extensive knowledge of a wide range of makes and models of vehicles and equipment. Crandall attended Wyoming Technical Institute for its automotive repair, chassis fabrication, and high-performance engine programs.

George Abraham is a materials scientist and manager of technical services at Allied High Tech Products, Inc. He has become an industry authority on metallography and authored numerous technical notes, articles, manuals, and presentations. He serves on the board of directors of the International Metallographic Society and the editorial board of the journal *Metallography, Microstructure, and Analysis*. Also appreciative of the art of metallography, Abraham has been known to get lost in microscopes, exploring the beauty of materials; his favorite microstructure is nodular cast iron. He has developed and taught materials seminars for 10 years and enjoys mentoring emerging professionals in science and engineering.

Anton Zadorozhnyy studied cognitive science at the University of California San Diego, receiving a degree in human–computer interaction, and delving into computational neuroscience, ethnography, and UX. He is part of LinkedIn's User Experience Design team and has helped shape UX for the Content, Search, Flagship, Learning, and Marketing Solutions products since 2013. He loves systems and storytelling. He immigrated to the United States from Ukraine and currently lives in Portland, OR.

Antoine Maas studied engineering in France at the University of Technology of Compiègne. He obtained a master of science in mechanical engineering with a specialization in noise and vibrations. Maas joined Dyson in 2012, and spent the first years of his career developing the acoustic innovation behind Dyson's first hair dryer, which is significantly quieter than the average hair dryer. It took him 6,593 tests to get the sound level of the Dyson Supersonic hair dryer right. He now researches cutting-edge acoustic technologies and applies them to Dyson's next generation of air-purifying fans. Maas is also a musician who takes active part in the UK's rich music scene.

Toby Nelson is a musician, programmer and audio engineer. As a musician, Toby works with recorded samples, analog synthesizers and software to produce abstract, experimental music and performs regularly in his music scene. He has and continues to release recordings both independently and through various record labels. His records have been consistently well-received by local press and independent music publications online. He has a bachelor's degree in computer science from Montana State University. He currently lives in Portland, Oregon with his partner and their cat, Muffin.

Amber Case grew up surrounded by technology. Her parents were broadcast engineers, and her father built microphones and speakers in his free time. Amber started recording and experimenting with tape at age six. Her obsession with sound grew into a lifelong mission, improving in quality as technologies advanced. She now uses experimental microphones and recording techniques to create avant-garde music and film. She frequently performs and exhibits sound design work, and has spoken about the future of sound design all over the world.

Amber speaks and consults globally with Fortune 500 companies on their product strategies, and how they can make technologies that work alongside humans. She is the author of *Calm Technology: Principles and Patterns for Non-Intrusive Design* (O'Reilly) and *An Illustrated Dictionary of Cyborg Anthropology* (CreateSpace). She's been listed among *Inc. Magazine*'s 30 under 30 and featured among *Fast Company*'s Most Influential Women in Technology. She has founded two startups, as well as CyborgCamp, a conference on the future of humans and technology.

Amber lives in Portland, OR. You can follow her on Twitter @caseorganic and learn more at *caseorganic.com*.

Aaron Day has been designing sound, experiences, and interfaces since 1998. He has worked for clients including Bruel & Kjaer, Fiat, Ferrari, Mozilla, Qoros, Telefónica, Bosch, Vodafone, Sprint, Siemens, Audi, and Samsung. A graduate of Reed College, Aaron began his career as a bicycle mechanic.

He lives with his family in Berlin, Germany.

Learn from experts.
Find the answers you need.

Sign up for a **10-day free trial** to get **unlimited access** to all of the content on Safari, including Learning Paths, interactive tutorials, and curated playlists that draw from thousands of ebooks and training videos on a wide range of topics, including data, design, DevOps, management, business—and much more.

Start your free trial at:
oreilly.com/safari

(No credit card required.)

Milton Keynes UK
Ingram Content Group UK Ltd.
UKHW020736200824
447159UK00009B/53

9 781491 961100